DK EYEWITNESS

Gardens
of the
World

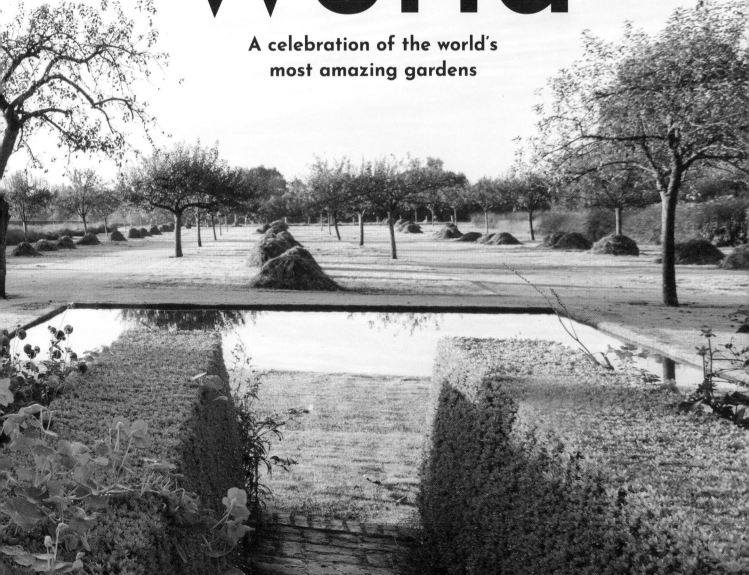

Gardens
of the
World

A celebration of the world's
most amazing gardens

CONTENTS

Previous page *A grande allée of apple trees at the center of Le Jardin Plume's Orchard Garden*

Clockwise from top

Monet's peaceful water garden in Giverny

The Eden Project's innovatively designed Rainforest Biome

The wild plantings of Le Jardin Plume

Impeccably crafted Buxus at the Hanging Gardens of Marqueyssac

Ambling through Jewel Changi Airport's unexpected paradise

Introduction

A Surrealist vision reclaimed by the jungle, the sprawling grounds of a royal palace, terraced gardens in the heart of an airport: incredible green spaces are all around us. It's little wonder people seek out gardens on their travels, be it touring the bucolic lands of the south of England, adding the great gardens of the US to a countrywide itinerary, or finding a moment of calm in Marrakesh's bustling center. And that's why we've created this book—to take you to the very places that stir the spirit and celebrate the beauty of nature.

The world is full of so many impeccable gardens, growing in the depths of jungles or sprouting from derelict ruins, that we've been spoiled for choice when compiling this book. So we've chosen those that tell a unique story, have been pivotal in the history of design, or are reinventing what it means to be a garden. Of course, you'll find the iconic—the powerful Versailles, the refined La Alhambra, and the futuristic Gardens by the Bay—but we've also included the inspirational, from a garden created out of grief to one that hoped to aid world peace. Innovation also shines in these pages, asking us to rethink what a garden can be. An underwater farm? It's possible, and it's here. A landscape that aims to unravel the curiosities of the universe? It's mind-bending, but it's marvelous.

We've organized this book by theme, so whether you value tradition and the order of a perfectly clipped hedge or the seeming chaos of an untamed landscape, there's a garden for you. That's not to say a garden is ever wholly ordered, wild, or mindful; each one is a blend of elements, and therein lies its appeal.

Some of the gardens in this book will be new to you and are very much absent on traditional tourist itineraries. Leaf through *Gardens of the World* and you'll soon unearth the wonderful gardens that lie beyond our own backyards, in every shape, size, and spirit. We're confident that you'll be inspired.

CAREFULLY
CURATED

When asked to think of the world's greatest gardens, it's the manicured landscapes that sit alongside baroque palaces, classical temples or ancient villas that spring to mind for most. These are the pristine gardens of elaborate parterres, ornate fountains and tree-lined avenues. Often involving decades' worth of planning, these gardens are an emphatic attempt to curate nature and create something splendid.

A PENCHANT FOR FASHION

Where once gardens served a highly practical purpose (think of medieval domestic gardens, for example), by the 13th century, the focus shifted to aesthetics. European gardens became symbolic of power, wealth, and position in society, with designs influenced by the fashion of the day. Versailles popularized the formal French style, drawing admirers from the world over who would return home hoping to mirror such intricacies on their own estates. Islamic gardens, meanwhile, were typically private places, not built to show off to outsiders. But they were no less opulent; centuries of gardens dictated that plantings were carefully arranged around water and signified spiritual and sensual nourishment.

Most formal gardens were certainly created to impress. Grand alleys led to royal mansions to evoke awe, and plants were grown in rows to impose order. Notable garden designers became known for their styles—André Le Nôtre's French formal, for one—and were desired commissions.

Yet being on trend has never been enough. Around the world, those with the means out-granded one another and the centuries that came before them. Gardens became more elaborate—the topiary extra sculpted, the trees taller, the statues rarer. Outrageous, palatial gardens were declarations of love, of power, and of status.

REDEFINING FORMALITY

Pushing the boundaries of formal design needn't mean increasing extravagance. There are always designers who blend and bend the rules: "Capability" Brown moved away from formality in favor of a naturalistic approach, while Vita Sackville-West crammed every inch of her English landscape with unfussy plantings.

What does precision planning mean, anyway? It may be less about symmetry and more about decades spent deciding where a bench should be placed, or putting in a year's worth of work to ensure tulips bloom for just a few weeks. Of course, precise planning goes into nearly every garden, but when it comes to meticulous curation, the gardens here are some of the best.

THE GARDENS OF VERSAILLES
FRANCE

HUMBLE ADMINISTRATOR'S GARDEN
CHINA

LONGWOOD GARDENS
US

SHALIMAR BAGH
INDIA

BLENHEIM PALACE GARDENS
UK

PORTLAND JAPANESE GARDEN
US

POWERSCOURT GARDENS
IRELAND

SUMMER PALACE
CHINA

KEUKENHOF
NETHERLANDS

HERRENHÄUSER GÄRTEN
GERMANY

VILLA D'ESTE
ITALY

SISSINGHURST CASTLE GARDEN
UK

THE HANGING GARDENS OF MARQUEYSSAC
FRANCE

LA ALHAMBRA
SPAIN

THE BOBOLI GARDENS
ITALY

DUMBARTON OAKS
US

Geometric paths, neat shrubberies, and a gleaming pool displaying exquisite symmetry in the formal gardens

The Gardens of Versailles

WHERE *Place d'Armes, Versailles* **WHEN** *Between late May and late October, when the fountains are played on certain days* **SIZE** *1,976 acres (800 hectares)*

A symbol of regal power, Versailles is the ultimate expression of nature dominated by man. Combining sweeping terraces and immaculate parterres, vast pools and grandiose fountains, razor-sharp hedges and topiary, this spectacular landscape exudes precision and panache.

At first encounter, Versailles is all about the palace. Yet beyond its golden gates and broad architectural sweep is an even more impressive creation—dazzling formal gardens that seem to go on forever. Everything feels oversized—statues tower over the landscape, avenues are disconcertingly wide, and vistas extend without limit. Versailles was designed to intimidate, and not just because of its scale.

The layout is so geometrically perfect; it is easy to wonder whether it is the work of human hands at all—a fitting reaction to gardens made for a godlike figure. Louis XIV, the self-named Sun King, was the most powerful monarch in Europe; he took as his inspiration and emblem the god Apollo, whose symbol was the sun. The gardens—filled with allusions to both through fountains, urns, and sunburst avenues—were a visual representation of Louis XIV's omnipotence. But they were also his most treasured creation and a tour de force of French garden art.

PAVING THE WAY

Louis XIV loved the city of Versailles so much, he decided to turn his father's royal hunting ground here into a royal château, the seat of French government. Royal gardener André Le Nôtre was commissioned to transform the site. It was a mammoth project; armies of laborers shifted tons of soil to create suitable terrain for lawns, parterres, and mature trees, thousands of which were uprooted from the nearby woods. Local villagers were evicted to provide the required land. Engineers diverted water from rivers and channeled it into the extravagant water features. Nothing was impossible. →

1661

Louis XIV launches a vast program of embellishment and expansion at Versailles, which he oversees until his death in 1715.

1664

The first of Louis's *fêtes*. Known as *Les Plaisirs de l'Île Enchantée*, the event lasts a whole week in May, concluding with a dazzling fireworks display.

1666

The fountains play for the first time.

1671

The Grand Canal is completed, projecting the garden further westward toward the setting sun.

1674

Louis XIV takes up residence at his vast new palace.

1774-1775

Louis XVI orders the replanting of most of the trees, because many are either dying or diseased.

1999

More than 10,000 trees on the grounds are wiped out in just one hour due to violent storms.

Top *Eighteen gold frogs spurting water toward Apollo's mother in the plush Latona Fountain*

Bottom *Le Nôtre's work, a supreme example of formal French garden style*

Le Nôtre proved an impeccable designer. He rooted the garden on an axis aligned with Louis's west-facing bedroom, with a view nothing short of spectacular. Closest to the palace, a terrace marked by two pools preluded fountains, sky-reflecting pools, and parterres, which all eventually led to the immense Grand Canal, into which the setting sun would dissolve.

TRY IT AT HOME

Planters

Perfect for topiarized evergreens, small trees, or shrubs, Versailles planters are a great way of adding French elegance to your garden. These wooden containers were designed for easy transportation of Versailles's citrus trees.

Versailles was to be a place of luxury, where Louis and his court could gather for events. Every inch was calculated to convey order and harmony: a defining trait of the fashionable French formal garden and a reflection of the decorum that courtiers were to show. Statues were placed with equidistant precision, each parterre had its twin, avenues ran parallel or diagonally from each other, or spread from a central point like the sun's rays. And, thanks to specialist staff, the gardens were kept in perfect condition. There were even full-time *terrassiers* to sand the paths.

TRICKS AND SURPRISES

Le Nôtre also shaped the land to create drama and surprise. At one point—thanks to a technique known as anamorphosis, whereby things are made to look different from a certain viewpoint— the Grand Canal appears larger than it is. When walking up the Royal Alley and standing at the foot of the Latona Staircase, the palace disappears, only to reemerge—as if by magic—a few steps later. Such effects were possible only thanks to Le Nôtre's mastery of perspective and optics.

Branching out from the main avenues, alleys led to secretive groves or *bosquets*, intimate garden "rooms" designed for small-scale court entertainments. Simpler *bosquets*, such as the Girandole Grove, feel like Parisian squares; others, like the Colonnade Grove, are more ostentatious.

PLAYING WITH WATER

The fountains were—and still are—Versailles's greatest glory. The most spectacular water features relate to Apollo. Appropriately, the magnificent Apollo Fountain is aligned with the king's view, at the end of the Royal Alley. Depicting a gilded Apollo emerging from the ocean on his chariot, it symbolizes the start of the day and Louis's famed daily awakening ceremony, known as the *levée* (rise).

To enjoy its full effect, Versailles should be seen with its fountains playing in summer. Apollo and his horses come alive as the water starts to froth and spray. And not to be missed is the Neptune Basin with its nearby Dragon Basin, both adorned with fantastical sea creatures. →

1

The length in miles (1.7 km) of the Grand Canal. It covers a surface of 56 acres (23 hectares)— that's nearly three times the size of the Place de la Concorde in Paris.

In Louis XIV's day, supply for the 1,400 fountains was a problem, despite cutting-edge engineering works. On grand occasions, garden boys would communicate to each other with whistles, turning taps on and off as and when necessary, to ensure fountains played as king and court walked past.

FOCUS ON

Water Frolics

Royal entertainment was not confined to admiring the water features; fun was also had on the water. Venetian gondolas and other ornamental ships were maintained at the head of the Grand Canal, where a shipyard was built alongside living quarters for gondoliers and carpenters. In 1671, the fleet was even given a captain.

Despite the incredible waterworks, many of the larger bodies of water were designed simply to stay still. These acted as giant sky- and sun-reflecting, space-expanding mirrors. Earth wasn't enough for the Sun King; his dominion stretched to the heavens, too. And why have one palace or fountain when it could be doubled in water?

CLOSE COLLABORATION

Versailles, of course, wasn't created overnight. It became a lifetime's project for Louis XIV, who continued to tweak and expand his gardens until his death in 1715. His collaboration with Le Nôtre was so successful, they became firm friends; Le Nôtre was approachable and direct and Louis appreciated this. Their friendship did not rule out the odd disagreement, however. Louis loved flowers; Le Nôtre hated them. As expected, the Sun King got his way. From his palace windows, he could admire colorful parterres filled with thousands of tulips (his favorite), daffodils, and many other blooms. Even in the depths of winter, Louis insisted on having flowers as well as fruit, the latter grown in the Potager du Roi, his enormous kitchen garden down the road.

A LASTING MASTERPIECE

Louis XIV walked around his beloved gardens as often as he could. He was so eager to make sure visitors didn't miss anything that he wrote a guidebook, *Manière de montrer les jardins de Versailles*. Concise and didactic, it features numbered instructions telling visitors the "appropriate" way to explore the gardens.

Louis's oft-repeated motto was *"L'état c'est moi"* (I am the state), but his self-symbolizing gardens showed him to be far more than that. He truly saw himself as the Sun—the firmament around which everything revolved, generator of beauty and harmony. For a time, Versailles—masterpiece of political propaganda—felt like the center of the world. Today, divested of its royal duties, the gardens of Versailles remain a tour de force, so powerful that the cliché is true—they really do take the breath away.

Clockwise
from top left
*Trellis
punctuated
with plants*

*Orange, lemon,
and palm trees
decorating
the Orangery
parterre*

*Precise
geometrical trees
lining straight
walking paths*

*Statues adorning
one of the lush
fountains*

CAREFULLY CURATED

Buildings, rocks, water, and plants forming the classical Chinese garden

Humble Administrator's Garden

WHERE *178 Dongbei Street, Gusu District, Suzhou* **WHEN** *May or September, on either side of the fiery summer, though Suzhou's gardens were designed to be appreciated in all seasons* **SIZE** *12 acres (5 hectares)*

A walled haven of high culture and lyrical beauty, the Humble Administrator's Garden remains a treasured relic of Ming dynasty refinement. To walk through this sprawling landscape is to embark on a journey through the ultimate expression of Chinese garden design.

As the Chinese proverb goes, "Above is heaven, below is Suzhou," pointing to the celebrated beauty of this historic region. Set amid the crisscrossing waterways of the Yangtze delta, Suzhou reached a peak of splendor and prosperity during the Ming dynasty (1368–1644). The city's wealthy scholar class built private gardens to show off their cultivated tastes, elevating garden art to new levels of aesthetic subtlety and refinement.

Of more than 60 Suzhou gardens surviving, one is considered the finest in all of southern China. It was first built in 1509 by the self-styled "Humble Administrator" Wang Xianchen, a retired official in the imperial civil service. Such was the garden's fame that artists of the day were frequent visitors, including painter and poet Wen Zhengming. Wen painted two albums of views and composed poetic odes to the garden,

a record that has helped preserve the garden's essential soul—even as sections of it were sold off and later rejoined over centuries of change.

THE ART OF GARDEN DESIGN

Wandering through the garden, over waterways and artificial hills and through corridors and pavilions, the view shifts with every step to reveal an orchestrated narrative in the manner of a Chinese landscape scroll painting. These elaborate art pieces, often yards long, were designed to be unfurled slowly, taking the viewer on a journey through meticulously detailed scenes, with paths or roads that lead the eye deeper into the work. This garden is no different: paths loop and zigzag languidly, encouraging contemplation and allowing the various spaces and scenes to be appreciated from new points of view. →

Open-sided buildings offer pause and sanctuary at scenic vantage points: the aptly named Pagoda Reflection Pavilion, the Stay and Listen Pavilion, the Far-Away-Looking Pavilion. Circular doorways, known as moon gates, and flower-shaped latticed windows are positioned to frame and crop exquisite vistas, revealing multiple layers of scenery intended to evoke a particular season, mood, or allegory.

ALL SEASONS AND SENSES

Along with architecture, rocks, and water, plants make up a key element of classical Chinese gardens, and those at the Humble Administrator's Garden are selected with the seasons in mind. Reddish-pink azaleas and peonies erupt in spring, jade-green lotuses and water lilies fill the ponds in summer, while fall to winter is a time for fragrant chrysanthemums, jasmine-like osmanthus, and delicate camellias.

The garden was certainly conceived as a place of pleasure to be savored at all points during the year, but not only with the eyes. In fall, the sound of the percussive pitter-patter of rain on bamboo can be appreciated in the Listening to the Sound of Rain Pavilion. The Lotus Breeze Pavilion, meanwhile, captures the fragrance of blooming lotuses in summer. It's said that the further the scent of lotus drifts, the sweeter it becomes. Lotuses, symbolic of virtue and purity, are the most prolific plant in the garden, which isn't surprising given that water makes up a fifth of its area.

WORLD IN MINIATURE

A playful use of scale is another key feature of classical Chinese garden design, reflecting a desire to reproduce China's vast natural and mythical landscapes within the comparatively small confines of a garden. Throughout the Humble Administrator's Garden, naturally eroded rocks known as *gongshi*, or "scholar's rocks," are carefully placed. Intricately weathered and textured, these are used to represent looming mountains. In the same way, certain ornamental trees like bonsai are selected for their ability to evoke much larger forest giants.

Surely the most delightful feature in the scale toolbox is *jiejing*, or "borrowed scenery." Suzhou's Beisi Pagoda, beyond the garden to the west, has been skillfully "borrowed" by the garden's designers. Particular pavilions and viewpoints frame the 249 ft (76 m) high pagoda to make it appear a part of the garden itself, vastly extending the scope of this idealized world. More remarkable still is that this illusion endures today even as modern Suzhou, with its mega malls and skyscrapers, rises ever higher beyond the city's protected historic core.

41

The number of buildings woven into the garden's overall design, reinforcing the idea that Chinese gardens are essentially built, not planted.

Clockwise from right

*Moon gates framing
pretty vignettes*

*Paths bordered
by neat trees and
complementary rocks
linking quaint pavilions*

*Fine magnolia blooming
in the garden*

IF YOU LIKE THIS

Lion's Grove Garden, Suzhou

CHINA · ASIA

This Yuan dynasty–era garden is defined by its displays of naturally gnarled and eroded limestone rocks taken from nearby Lake Tai.

Lingering Garden, Suzhou

CHINA · ASIA

A long covered corridor weaves together four themed sections of this garden, dominated by fine architecture dating to the Qing dynasty (1644–1912).

CAREFULLY CURATED

Longwood Gardens

WHERE *1001 Longwood Road, Kennett Square, Pennsylvania* **WHEN** *Winter, when the garden becomes more subdued, and holiday-themed events take place* **SIZE** *1,100 acres (445 hectares)*

Influenced by the great gardens of Europe and the beauty of southeastern Pennsylvania, Longwood Gardens is an epic showcase of horticultural prestige featuring formal gardens, breathtaking conservatories, and fountains galore, all carefully curated to reflect the seasons.

In Pennsylvania's Brandywine Valley sits this expansive garden, equally rich in history and beauty. If the soil could talk, extraordinary stories of the past would be told—like those of the Lenni Lenape Nation, the Indigenous peoples of what is now eastern Pennsylvania whose ancestors lived here; or of enslaved people who crossed over the paths of the land to be led to safety via the Underground Railroad. Fast-forward to today, and the plot is home to a garden that is world-renowned.

THE GARDEN'S ROOTS

Longwood is the crown jewel of 36 gardens within 30 miles (48 km) of Philadelphia, a region known as America's Garden Capital. The state of Pennsylvania, founded by English Quaker leader and colonist William Penn, translates to "Penn's woods"; it's fitting, then, that woods are the very reason Longwood Gardens exist. In 1700, Quaker farmer George Peirce purchased the land now occupied by Longwood, and in the late 18th century, his descendants planted an arboretum, which became one of the nation's greatest collection of trees. By the late 19th century, however, the Peirce family allowed the collection to deteriorate, leaving it susceptible to lumber companies. In 1906, industrialist Pierre Samuel du Pont could not bear to see this former marvel cut down and chose to buy it as a country estate to preserve the trees. →

The Main Fountain Garden putting on an impressive water display

FOCUS ON

Lenape Nation

The Lenni Lenape Indigenous peoples hunted the forests and planted the fields of the land where Longwood stands for thousands of years before it was acquired by the Quakers.

Stunning blooms and planting arrangements in Longwood's East Conservatory

Du Pont didn't just hope to restore the land to its former condition—he was also keen to create a place where he could entertain his friends. A self-taught garden designer and well-traveled man with means, he possessed the creative and financial ability to curate a horticultural dream world and set to work.

THE GARDENS COME TO LIFE

Du Pont's planned entertaining space certainly remains to this day: Longwood's outdoor and 20 indoor spaces dazzle with events and festivals in every season. Longwood has mastered the art of having its plants bloom at the perfect time for maximum impact, and nothing showcases this more perfectly than

the Spring Blooms display in April. The main conservatory comes alive with cymbidium orchids, African violets, and tens of thousands of spring bulbs like amaryllis and freesias. At the same time, a tapestry of daffodils, tulips, and forsythias color the outdoor gardens, perfuming the air with a subtle fragrance. The fountains, too, emerge from their winter slumber, delighting visitors in the Italian Water Garden.

Water defines the summer season, too, with the famous Festival of Fountains. Balmy summer evenings are set to the soundtrack of live music and liquid fireworks soaring 175 ft (50 m) high in the Main Fountain Garden. During the day, vibrant colors shine in the rectangular beds in the Rose Garden, overlooking the fountain.

A WONDERFUL TIME OF YEAR

The heady joys of spring and summer tend to be a garden's defining glory, but not so here. Fall's bounty is celebrated with Autumn's Colors, when visitors will stumble across glossy nuts, brilliant berries, and curiously shaped acorns on crisp walks across the property. Combine this with spectacularly painted

5,000

The number of orchids in Longwood's Orchid Extravaganza display. It takes around 65 staff members and volunteers to create the intricate display.

vistas and fall may just be the perfect season here—were it not for winter, where fun is the seasonal priority. A Longwood Christmas sees families marvel at the festive planting scheme—trees with fiery red tones and poinsettias in the conservatory—accompanied by lights and organ notes, while Winter Wonder celebrates the subdued colors and snowcapped trees in the outdoor gardens.

The design process and gardening techniques may vary year on year, but special care is always taken to achieve the perfect set piece—one that honors the uniqueness of each season. What is Longwood, this extravagant horticultural wonderland, if not du Pont's grand vision to delight and dazzle those who visit?

Left *Dainty yellow and pink tulips gracing the landscape in the spring*

Right *Snow settling on the topiary in the outdoor gardens in the winter*

Shalimar Bagh

WHERE *Dal Lake, Srinagar, Jammu, and Kashmir* WHEN *April is an ideal month to visit, to coincide with the famous Srinagar tulip festival* SIZE *32 acres (13 hectares)*

Snowcapped peaks provide the spectacular backdrop for Shalimar Bagh. Laid out on great terraces rising up from Dal Lake, this 17th-century garden displays the exquisite patterning, abundant water features, and sensuous charms of Persian-inspired landscape design.

The ultimate joy of Shalimar Bagh is its location. Close to the beauties of Dal Lake, and backed by the drama of the Himalayan foothills, this is a garden treasured as much for the glorious views it offers as its sophisticated designs. As soon as you set foot inside this wondrous Mughal garden, you are captivated.

AN IMPERIAL GARDEN

The Mughal emperors saw the fertile valley of Kashmir as a paradise on earth and a welcome retreat from the hot, arid plains of their capital, some 500 miles (800 km) further south. It was here in 1619 that the fourth Mughal emperor Jahangir (1569-1627) and his son Shah Jahan (1592-1666) began work on their imperial pleasure garden.

Shalimar Bagh was inspired by Persian style—a flat, geometric layout divided into fourfold patterns by axial waterways. Shalimar's sloping location, however, sets it apart from other gardens of its ilk, allowing for the central channel to cascade down the hillside. Fed by natural springs, it provided irrigation for the garden's many fruit orchards and scented flower gardens of jasmine, crocus, rose, lilac, and violet.

This central channel connects the garden's three terraces, which form a steady uphill progression from the shores of Dal Lake to a peaceful mountain sanctuary. The first of these terraces is where the emperor—enthroned in the pink pavilion—heard petitions from his subjects. The middle terrace was a sumptuous garden reserved for the pleasure of the court, with a pavilion—of which only the foundations remain—for private audiences. The uppermost terrace was a secluded garden reserved for the private use of the empress and her ladies. In many ways, this final terrace is the culmination of Shalimar Bagh, offering exquisite views from its Black Pavilion, which appears to float on the surrounding pool.

No longer an exclusive pleasure ground for emperors, today this imperial garden can be enjoyed by anyone. Restoration work is underway to repair its architecture—the fountains and cascades work again; the planting is increasingly plentiful and sensuous. Given Kashmir's political instability, Shalimar Bagh is not always an easy place to visit. But, like the Mughal emperors of old, you may find that it is a place you long to return to.

Right *The Zabarwan mountains looming high above the terraces*

Below *A row of fountains leading to the restored Black Pavilion*

FOCUS ON

Nur Jahan

Shalimar Bagh (meaning "abode of love") was created as a symbol of Emperor Jahangir's love for his 20th, and some say favorite, wife, Nur Jahan. She was born into Persian aristocracy, and her charisma, intelligence, and fearlessness made her a powerful figure at court.

IF YOU LIKE THIS

Nishat Bagh

INDIA · ASIA

Adjacent to Shalimar Bagh, the serenely beautiful Nishat Bagh (translated as "garden of delight") is another stunning Mughal garden, featuring glistening water chutes and zodiac-inspired terraces.

Top
*Vanbrugh's
Grand Bridge
spanning the
artificially
created lake*

Bottom *The
formal upper
water terrace*

Blenheim Palace Gardens

WHERE *Blenheim Palace, Woodstock, Oxfordshire* **WHEN** *September and October, to appreciate the warm fall colors of Capability Brown's trees in and around the parkland*
SIZE *2,409 acres (974 hectares)*

The gardens of Blenheim Palace are the unsurpassed legacy of Lancelot "Capability" Brown, whose name is synonymous with the 18th-century English landscape garden style. Brown's seemingly natural but highly contrived landscape has long been admired as his finest work.

Set in the heart of the English countryside, the Blenheim Palace Gardens are a national treasure—much like the designer at its helm, Capability Brown. Britain's most influential landscape designer, Brown moved away from traditional formal gardens in favor of a more naturalistic approach. It is his work at Blenheim that ensures its place on the international garden stage.

FRENCH FORMALITY

Though it's heavily associated with Brown and the English garden style today, Blenheim wasn't always so. Blenheim Palace, created for the 1st Duke of Marlborough (1650–1722), was built at a time when taking design ideas from French courts was all the rage. When architect Sir John Vanbrugh, royal gardener Henry Wise, and garden designer George London started work on the palace gardens, they implemented arresting avenues that disappeared into the distance and formal beds containing many clipped pyramidal yews. On the south side of the house, a geometric raised parterre was supported by high walls with rounded bastions. Outside the parterre, straight paths cut through dense plantations.

Decades later, however, this French style was considered outdated and expensive to maintain, and was rivaled by the English naturalistic style, spearheaded by the man of the moment: Brown. In 1763, George Spencer, the 4th Duke of Marlborough (1739–1817), commissioned Brown to transform the garden into this fashionable new style. →

3,000

The number of yew trees planted in 1987 to create the Blenheim maze. The design was inspired by the military trophies located on the palace's roof.

TRANSFORMATIVE DESIGN

Brown has often been painted as a destroyer of formality, but he simply saw the "capabilities" of a site (hence, his nickname). When he came to Vanbrugh's ornate bridge, for instance, spanning the Glyme River, Brown didn't demolish it. Instead, he dammed the river to create a lake in perfect proportion with the bridge. The view of this from the nearby Triumphal Gate in Woodstock village remains one of the most beautiful of any English landscape and a defining example of naturalistic design.

FOCUS ON

Lancelot Brown

Born in Northumberland, Brown (1716–1783) worked as a gardener's apprentice at Kirkharle Hall after finishing school. He then joined the staff at Stowe gardens, working under William Kent, one of the founders of the new English style of garden, before being made head gardener. From 1750, he worked independently, and transformed over 250 landscapes in England.

Indeed, Brown's signature style was to create a landscape that looked like it had been there all along but was in fact an overlay of what was already there. To do so, he relied on tested elements. Carefully positioned trees would conceal, reveal, and enhance features. One of his trademarks was expensive Lebanese Cedar, which he planted close to the house to frame it within its landscape. He replaced the French formal gardens with a closely cut lawn that came right up to the front door—a feature most desirable at the time. Formal avenues were dismantled, too, by removing sections to expose expanses of grass and open up views. Such work took a huge amount of labor, but the results are seamless; the garden appears to lack boundaries.

A CONTINUED VISION

While Blenheim and Brown go hand in hand, not everything is his work. The celebrated water parterre, laid out by the French landscape architect Achille Duchêne for the 9th Duke of Marlborough, hints at the garden's original formality, where ornate water basins and low box hedging were designed to be admired from the palace windows. The Italian Garden also dazzles with hedges of golden yews and a fountain. Brown's own work was dominated by water, so it seems fitting that if formality was to be restored here, it was with water at its heart.

Despite these later ornate touches, what Brown did with the landscape reigns supreme. Seen from Vanbrugh's bridge, Brown's planting precision is evident—he knew how his trees would frame key features and how to copy nature in such a way that it looked organic. His enduring legacy at Blenheim cannot be denied.

Clockwise from right

A 300-year-old Lebanese Cedar in the grounds

Pristine lawns surrounding the palace

Dense vegetation lining the Secret Garden, the 10th Duke of Marlborough's private garden

Portland Japanese Garden

WHERE *611 SW Kingston Avenue, Portland, Oregon* **WHEN** *Spring brings bright blooms, while fall dazzles with golden colors* **SIZE** *12 acres (5 hectares)*

Heralded as the most authentic Japanese garden outside Japan, the Portland Japanese Garden is a meticulously crafted showpiece of design. Winding paths, calming waters, and verdant plantings induce tranquility—a true embodiment of Japanese landscaping and principles.

Born out of a hope for healing between two World War II adversaries—the US and Japan—the Portland Japanese Garden has put peace and unity at its heart since inception. Indeed, this garden, carved from a native Pacific Northwest forest and maintained by Japanese gardeners since its inception in 1963, sees local plants like shore pine *(Pinus contorta)* and Douglas fir *(Pseudotsuga menziesii)* coexist with Japanese black pine *(Pinus thunbergiana)* and red pine *(Pinus densiflora)*—a symbolic connection between two cultures, if ever there was one.

INTENTIONALITY

When Japanese landscape architect Takuma Tomo was tasked with designing a space where Americans could connect with Japanese ideals, he chose not to focus on a single style like classic Japanese gardens do. Instead, he divided the space into five distinct areas to reflect the developments in Japanese garden aesthetics.

Paths and bridges cross carp-filled pools in the Strolling Pond Garden, designed for wandering; raked gravel and sand fill the Sand and Stone Garden, built to encourage contemplation; a ceremonial teahouse lies at the heart of the Tea Garden, historically a space to detach from the hectic everyday. The Natural Garden and Flat Garden, meanwhile, were both designed to show off their changes through the seasons. Throughout, all of the main elements of Japanese garden design blend harmoniously: water, stone, bridges, fences, trees, and flowers.

High standards have been maintained through the decades, under the care of successive curators. Trimming a tree or moving a stone is not done unthinkingly; each action is a delicate process that ensures authenticity. Yet being here is less about the plants—there are no plant labels—and more about the experience. What started as an olive branch has been crafted into a place of beauty, one to fill heart and spirit.

Clockwise from right

*A golden hue taking over
the Strolling Pond Garden
in the fall*

*Weeping cherry trees
flowering in the spring in
the Flat Garden*

*Pergolas inviting serene
walks through the garden*

IF YOU LIKE THIS

Shinjuku Gyoen National Garden

JAPAN · ASIA

Of the three different
types that comprise this
garden, the traditional
Japanese landscape
garden is the most
picturesque. Ponds
dotted with bridges
provide calming views,
well-manicured trees
surround the water, and
a pretty collection of
wisteria, cherry trees, and
azaleas blooms in spring.

Top *Water surging from the fountain in Triton Lake*

Bottom *The Walled Garden's long, colorful double borders in summer*

IRELAND · EUROPE

Powerscourt Gardens

WHERE *Powerscourt Demesne, Enniskerry, Co. Wicklow* **WHEN** *Spring, when azaleas grace the Japanese garden; and summer, when colors flourish in the Walled Garden* **SIZE** *47 acres (19 hectares)*

Set against a dramatic backdrop of mountains, the ornamental gardens of Powerscourt Estate are the embodiment of 19th-century style and splendor. The divine blend of formal elements, including sculpture and topiary with flower borders and ponds, are a triumph.

There are few views that can compare to the one from the top terrace of Powerscourt, where a broad vista stretches out across sculpted terraces to the water and beyond, to the Sugarloaf Mountain. Creating such an incredible scene took many years, architects, and laborers, as well as the directions of the 6th and 7th Viscounts Powerscourt, who are responsible for much of the garden's present form.

During the 19th century, both viscounts took a trip known as the Grand Tour through Europe, where they plucked ideas from the great gardens they saw. As a result, this is a landscape of variety. Naturally, Powerscourt contains elements of Baroque-style landscape compositions, as seen at Versailles: sweeping views, geometric layouts, masses of statuary. From the top terrace, the Perron—an Italianate double stairway—leads down to the Italian Garden, where elegant manicured lawns are inset with neat beds of bright annuals and presided over by stately marble sculptures of Roman

gods. Below, Triton Lake adds dynamism, lorded over by a fountain spurting water high into the air—an energy that is drawn back in the nearby Walled Garden, where Ireland's largest herbaceous border blooms in summer.

Moving further out, the garden becomes intentionally more informal, allowing it to gradually blend out into the wider landscape. Yet, surprises still await: the Japanese Garden dazzles with pretty bridges; the mossy Grotto thrills with Gothic mystery; and the Tower Valley stuns with its Pepperpot Tower, nestled among the evergreens. As the trail loops back to the top terrace, it offers a final, lingering look at that view.

100

The number of workers it is said to have taken to create the Italian Garden terraces, which took more than 12 years to construct using only shovels and spades.

IF YOU LIKE THIS

Villa Barbarigo

ITALY · EUROPE

The gardens of Villa Barbarigo in Valsanzibio have all the impressive trappings of Baroque design, including ornate gates, steps and follies, clipped evergreens, statues, vistas, and pools. There's also a sense of fun, with trick fountains that soak visitors when they least expect it, a rabbit island, and a maze.

Summer Palace

WHERE *19 Xinjian Gongmen, Haidian District, Beijing* **WHEN** *April and May to see magnolia and cherry trees in bloom; September is the best month to visit for warm weather and clear skies* **SIZE** *734 acres (297 hectares)*

A glorious *mise en scène* of human-made hills, lakes and islets, vaulted arch bridges, and sumptuous palace buildings on a truly epic scale, the Summer Palace is a living monument to the power, wealth, and refinement of China's last imperial dynasty.

Classical Chinese gardens recreate idealized landscapes in miniature, but the sprawling Summer Palace is anything but small. The sheer size of this gilded retreat—the largest imperial garden in the world—sets it apart. Three quarters of its area is covered by the mirror-still Kunming Lake. Longevity Hill, raised from the soil excavated from the lake, rises some 196 ft (60 m) above the water and is crowned by the octagonal Tower of Buddhist Incense plus a retinue of majestic halls and pavilions. The result is a stunning scene that greets every visitor to pass through the towering portal of the East Palace Gate.

A GARDEN FIT FOR AN EMPRESS

Before the collapse of imperial China between 1911 and 1912, the Summer Palace was the private domain of China's rulers. Among its last royal residents was Cixi, the Empress Dowager, who restored the gardens in the 1880s and named the vast complex Yiheyuan, the Garden of Preserving Harmony. The Summer Palace today is like a time capsule of that age. Cixi's throne room and private chambers remain much as she left them, the elegant courtyards embellished with ornamental rocks and planted with her coral-pink crab apple trees to symbolize honor and health.

Beyond Cixi's quarters, the Inviting the Moon Gate opens onto the Long Corridor, an elegant canopied walkway inset with pavilions that skirts the north shore of the lake. It's easy to imagine Cixi taking a stroll here, enjoying the breeze off the water and admiring the many artworks that adorn every crossbeam and ceiling arch—paintings of pastoral scenes, Buddhist stories, myths, and folk tales. →

Right *Giant water lily pads floating on Kunming Lake*

Far right *Intricate architectural details at the Summer Palace*

TIMELINE OF EVENTS

1764

The Summer Palace, then called the Garden of Clear Ripples, is built by Qing emperor Qianlong as a birthday gift to his mother.

1860

British and French troops raid and loot the Summer Palace and neighboring gardens during the Second Opium War.

1888

Empress Cixi rebuilds the Summer Palace, naming it the Garden of Preserving Harmony.

1914

After the fall of the Qing Dynasty, the Summer Palace opens to the public for the first time.

Left *The 17-Arch Bridge connecting one area of Kunming Lake with an islet*

Right *Spring brings a delicate dusting of pink blossoms*

THE WAY OF WIND AND WATER

As in most classical Chinese gardens, or in any garden for that matter, plants are just a single component of the Summer Palace. Water and landscape features, ornamental rocks, art, and architecture all play their part. Successfully balancing these elements is key to Chinese garden design. Feng shui, the "way of the wind and water," is the ancient Chinese art of arranging an environment in order to achieve harmony and peace. Peace, in this sense, is obtained through dutiful observance of the Taoist concept of yin and yang, the principle of complementary forces. Longevity Hill and Kunming Lake are the perfect illustration of this concept: the water represents yin as a calm, yielding element, while mountains, vertical and powerful, are the opposing yang. The Garden of Harmonious Interests is another example, though perhaps on a more manageable scale. Its individual features come together in delightful harmony: trickling water features, ornamental bridges, gentle optical illusions, calligraphy and paintings, a miniature Long Corridor, and plantings like lotuses and willows that reflect the changes of the seasons.

FANTASY AND FOLLIES

The Summer Palace is imbued with symbolism. Many of its features allude to famous scenes in China, such as Hangzhou's West Lake or the

gardens of Suzhou. But the Summer Palace also came to symbolize how out of touch China's rulers had become. The most potent example is Cixi's Marble Boat, a two-story pavilion styled in the shape of a Western-style paddle steamer. To rebuild the gardens as a whole, Cixi used funds earmarked for a new Chinese navy. At the time, China needed modern warships to stand up to colonial powers. Instead, it got a single, immovable boat made of stone.

2,388

The length in feet (728 m) of the Long Corridor, the Summer Palace's covered lakeside walkway.

A GARDEN FOR POSTERITY

Fittingly, the Chinese character "shou," meaning long life or longevity, is inscribed on buildings throughout the garden. While the Summer Palace saw the closing chapter of 2,000 years of imperial tradition and the end of the Qing dynasty's reign, the imperial gardens lived on. Two years after the abdication of the last emperor, the complex was opened to the public, a powerful symbol of emancipation to the citizens of the new Chinese republic. And it has remained open, barring a few hiccups, ever since. In 1998, the Summer Palace was designated a World Heritage Site, a further step toward cementing the longevity hoped for during its creation centuries earlier.

Empress Dowager Cixi's elaborate Marble Boat

Keukenhof

WHERE *Stationsweg 166A, Lisse* **WHEN** *Late March until mid-May only, with the first ranks of tulips in full bloom by the fourth week of opening* **SIZE** *86 acres (35 hectares)*

Preparation is everything at the Keukenhof, where gardeners spend most of the year planning and perfecting a short-lived but spectacular floral fantasia. Beds are nurtured to perfection, allowing colorful blooms to flow through the lawns of the world's most famous tulip nursery.

For just a couple of months in spring, the flat bulb fields of the Bollenstreek (Flower Strip), a 30-mile (48 km) stretch of fertile farmland, erupt into color. Purple and orange crocuses are first to burst from thawing soil, followed by daffodils and narcissi, hyacinths and irises. But the tulips steal the show at Keukenhof, the garden at the very heart of the Bollenstreek.

ONE BULB AT A TIME

Keukenhof was an English-style garden until 1949, when commercial bulb growers spotted its potential as a showcase for their products. Upon opening in 1950, it became more than a business venture, drawing in 236,000 people who came to admire its transient beauties. By 2019, 1.4 million visitors were jostling for the perfect photograph. And it's clear what all the fuss is about—this garden is pure precision.

A flower bulb park as meticuloulsly ordered as Keukenhof does not simply rise from the soil on its own. With millions of bulbs to be planted by hand, one by one, creating such a flower show is a hard, painstaking labor. For each bulb to bloom in sequence, ensuring a continuous display, it must be planted to the right depth and meticulously distanced to achieve maximum impact. No sooner has the blooming season ended than work begins on next year's displays. A showpiece for Dutch floral wizardry, Keukenhof in its brilliant, brief, headily scented spring never fails to captivate.

TRY IT AT HOME

Tulip Fever

You don't need a vast estate to plant tulips. In fact, for the urban Dutch, the tulip is a flower to be grown in pots and window boxes. Buy pedigree bulbs at Keukenhof's on-site shops, where experts will advise how and when to plant.

Clockwise from top
Row upon row of brightly colored tulips in full bloom

Dedicated gardeners planting bulbs between October and the end of December, to bloom the following spring

Pretty beds of pink and blue hyacinths

The immaculate Great Garden in front of Schloss Herrenhausen

Herrenhäuser Gärten

WHERE *Herrenhäuser Straße 4, Hanover* **WHEN** *April to October, when performing arts events like concerts and festivals are held and the water features are turned on* **SIZE** *334 acres (135 hectares)*

An embodiment of aristocratic elegance, the Herrenhausen Gardens are a masterful mix of parterres, tree-lined avenues, water features, and gilded statues. The crowning glory, the Great Garden at the center, forms one of the most important Baroque gardens in Europe.

Formal, fancy, and of immense proportions, Herrenhäuser Gärten stands as a reminder of an age that has since passed, offering its visitors the same leisurely promenade that was once reserved for royalty and their noble guests. The grandiose estate, made up of four gardens surrounding a palace, was known among courtiers and nobility in the 17th, 18th, and 19th centuries for its masked balls amid glittering greenery and gondola rides on the canal that frames the Great Garden. Today, the gardens remain a place of pleasure, their synchronized fountains and cultural events still drawing in crowds.

THE BEGINNINGS OF A LEGACY

Dating back more than 300 years, the fine Royal Gardens of Herrenhausen owe their existence to Electress Sophia, wife to Ernest Augustus, Prince-Elector of Hanover. Alongside master gardener Martin Charbonnier, Sophia supervised the palace garden's development—an expansion of the original pleasure garden on the estate half of its present size. She took inspiration from the grandest gardens of France—Versailles and Vaux-le-Vicomte—as well as Het Loo Palace in the Netherlands, the country in which she grew up.

It was the aptly named Great Garden (Großer Garten) that Sophia dedicated most time to, working on it for three decades until her death in 1714. With Charbonnier, she laid down strict geometric patterns with intricate swirls, miles of hornbeam and box hedges, and the tallest water fountain in Europe, the Great Fountain, reaching an impressive 236 ft (72 m) high. She introduced rare plants and commissioned master sculptors to produce artistry befitting a royal garden. Sophia was passionately devoted to her work, reportedly summing up her commitment in a comment: "The garden is my life." →

25,000

The number of orchids cultivated at Herrenhäuser Gärten. About 3,000 of these are different orchid species, with another 1,000 hybrid varieties.

A BOTANICAL MASTERPIECE

Beyond the 124 acres (50 hectares) that make up the Great Garden, Herrenhäuser Gärten is home to three other garden marvels: Berggarten, Welfengarten, and Georgengarten, each one as impressive as the next. Across from the Great Garden, the Berggarten started life as a garden to grow crops. However, given her vast interest in rare plants, Sophia transformed the area into a botanical garden where she could cultivate and care for species from around the world.

Sophia's veritable paradise was added to and reworked over the centuries, but her desire for a riot of colors and beauty has always been honored. A prairie garden blooms in late summer, with more than 900 flowering shrubs and diverse grasses from North America. Cactus, rainforest, subtropical, and tropical display gardens, meanwhile, occupy the hothouses and release their perfumed essential oils under the sun. There are separate displays of irises, rhododendrons, and magnolias, as well as a bountiful flower meadow and a stately stone garden. Here, too, is one of the largest collections of orchids in the world.

ENGLISH LANDSCAPES

If the Berggarten is a journey through the world, Welfengarten and Georgengarten are firmly rooted in the English landscape style. In the eastern portion of Herrenhäuser Gärten lies Herrenhäuser Allee, a 1.2-mile (2 km) long avenue lined with four rows of linden (*Tilia*) trees, linking the Great Garden with the city of Hanover. Flanking either side of this avenue is Georgengarten, whose appearance is akin

to a landscape painting. This public park, laid out in the 18th century, lies in strict contrast to the formal Great Garden, its lush green lawns, tranquil lakes, shrubberies, and ornamental bridges setting the scene for relaxed strolls and picnics. Toward the city end of the alley, Welfengarten is just as reminiscent of English-style gardens, with grand Welfenschloss at its center.

FOCUS ON

Garden Guests

At its peak, Herrenhausen played host to many important guests: Peter the Great, tsar of Russia, who danced here with Sophia; the great composer George Frideric Handel, who performed here; Gottfried Wilhelm Leibniz, the German philosopher, of whom Sophia was a friend and confidant; as well as many artists, poets and writers.

Sophia's was not the only influence that shaped Herrenhäuser Gärten; indeed, successors came and went, and bombings during World War II resulted in refurbishments. Today, the complex's ensemble of meticulously preserved gardens combines old with new, historic with modernist. No matter what, Herrenhäuser Gärten is a true expression of garden art and a treasure trove of botanical diversity that never fails to amaze thousands of visitors every year.

Clockwise
from top left

*Admiring the
theatrical
Great Fountain*

*Fallen
auburn leaves
carpeting
Herrenhäuser
Allee*

*Trees reflected
in the still
waters of the
Georgengarten*

Villa d'Este

WHERE *Piazza Trento 5, Tivoli* **WHEN** *In the height of summer, when the cooling spray*
of the many fountains and the dappled shade of the evergreens counteract the heat
SIZE *11 acres (4.5 hectares)*

The fine Villa d'Este is a unique example of a 16th-century Italian High Renaissance garden.
Born out of disillusionment, this pristine landscape was the first and most extravagant
iconographic garden to use water as its primary element.

The role of fountains as a symbol of power and status has been understood for centuries, but the use of water reached a new level at the height of the Italian Renaissance. This period's revival of classical models hugely influenced humankind's relationship with nature, with gardens becoming grander, inspired by order, and filled with features that showed off the wealth of their owners.

Indeed, the gravity-fed aquatic theatrics at the Villa d'Este—water powering musical instruments and roaring over cascades—were inspired by the Cardinal Ippolito II d'Este, one of the most wealthy ecclesiastics of the 16th century. After his failed bid for the papacy, he accepted the governorship of the hill town of Tivoli and created a sumptuous country residence. With the aid of architect and antiquarian Pirro Ligorio, he consoled himself by creating a water-inspired garden like no other, with the sole purpose of glorifying himself and impressing visitors. That, he did. In the spirit of the playfulness of the High Renaissance garden, networks of pipes connected to pressure pads activated random jets of water—*giochi d'aqua*, or water jokes—that made unsuspecting passersby squeal with a mixture of horror and delight. Yet, as well as thrilling visitors, the villa became the blueprint for later High Baroque gardens that took hydraulic theatricality to new heights.

PRECISE PLANNING

The gardens were built on a steep terraced western slope, with a central axis running up through the terraces toward the villa, which appears almost suspended at its summit. →

View from the Neptune Fountain over peaceful fish ponds surrounded by potted citrus trees

IF YOU LIKE THIS

Villa Lante
ITALY · EUROPE

A well-preserved High Renaissance garden in the town of Bagnaia, the Villa Lante was created by Cardinal Gianfrancesco Gambara and designer Giacomo Barozzi da Vignola from 1568. Highlights include the Water Chain that evokes the sounds of a mountain stream and the ingenious Fountain of the Table, where water flows along the length of a table; this acted as a wine cooler as guests dined.

Clockwise from top

The 1930s Neptune Fountain stealing the show with its dramatic water displays

Commanding views from the villa over Tivoli

Jets and spouts—up to 300—lining the Avenue of One Hundred Fountains

Following this axis is a long, straight central stairway flanked by high hedges of laurel. The original entrance into this watery oasis was through an unassuming little door at the lowest level, from where guests had a view up to the magnificent villa as they ascended. Today, the view of the garden takes center stage; access is now through the ornate rooms of the villa, allowing visitors to admire the symmetry of the gardens from above before descending. Nonetheless, one of the most marvelous features remains near the original entrance: the Rotunda of the Cypresses, a grove of ancient cypress trees around a circular space.

A WONDER GARDEN

The garden unfolds through a sequence of symmetrical garden "rooms," with short flights of steps and straight paths leading to alcoves and niches occupied by classical deities. Each terrace is marked by a different use of water, producing a symphony of sounds to accompany a stroll. Whether splashing, falling, or trickling, the fountains at the Villa d' Este can be likened to the performance of an aquatic orchestra.

Past the cypress rotunda, huge displays stun at the majestic Neptune Fountain. The sheer volume and power of the rising water columns meeting the curtain of water coming down is highly dramatic, enhanced by a rainbow playing in the spray. Above and behind, the Fountain of the Organ uses air and water pressure to produce musical notes—still a novelty centuries later.

As well as water, the use of limited elements such as stonework and evergreens remains a constant in the garden. The dark, shady groves and clipped fresh green hedging of yew are valued for their texture and shape but, more importantly, provide a contrasting backdrop for the many statues scattered over the grounds.

ENDURING VISION

Like most historic gardens, the villa suffered a period of decline, from 1695. Yet the imitation of the 18th-century English Landscape style, which obliterated many formal Renaissance gardens, passed the Villa d'Este by. This benign neglect preserved the garden's integrity and originality, enabling the Italian state to restore and reimagine the cardinal's vision.

Looking down from the upper terrace, views of the garden fall away and reach out for miles over the Roman countryside. This breathtaking vista is exactly the effect the cardinal intended to achieve—a vision that would enthrall visitors and inspire many gardens to come.

Top Rosa
mulliganii
tumbling over
the pergola in
the White
Garden

Bottom
Spring blooms
in the South
Cottage
Garden

Next page
A plant-
covered wall
dividing the
"rooms"

Sissinghurst Castle Garden

WHERE *Biddenden Road, Cranbrook, Kent* WHEN *May–June, when the garden is at its most spectacular and the irises and roses are in full bloom* SIZE *450 acres (182 hectares)*

It is said that love conquers all, and that was certainly the case for Vita Sackville-West and Harold Nicholson who, in 1930, fell in love with this derelict Kentish manor. Together they worked tirelessly to achieve their vision of a poetic English country garden.

The garden at Sissinghurst has it all—a rare alchemy of history, personality, passion, and plants, making it a place of pilgrimage for garden lovers the world over. Entering through the red-brick Tudor arch feels like taking a thrilling peek into a private Eden, a world of artful beauty in which beds are crammed full to the brim with profusions of delicate blooms and the air is fragranced with floral scents.

What makes Sissinghurst unique, however, is the talented and somewhat unconventional couple who created it from little more than an agricultural dump, writer and poet Vita Sackville-West and her husband, diplomat and diarist Harold Nicholson. Theirs was a partnership of talents in which Vita was the artist and Harold the architect. Vita had a strong visual sensibility, forged in part by her aristocratic background and passion for Renaissance Italy. Harold supported her artistry

with his astute eye for geometry and symmetry. He brought clarity to the whole by resolving awkward angles and perspectives in carefully considered garden "rooms" contained within walls or hedges, creating the perfect framework for Vita's luscious plantings.

MORE IS MORE

Vita was no minimalist. "Cram, cram, cram, every chink and cranny," was her motto. And cram she did. Her layered beds were dense with thick underplanting and chock-full with lavish groupings. No space went unused. Even the garden walls, the ruins of an Elizabethan manor that once stood here, are home to an array of well-trained climbers, vines, and tumbling roses. Though her unfussy style may appear sporadic and unconventional, Vita had an extraordinary vision, one that set the standard for English country gardens throughout the 20th century. →

Clockwise from top

Wisteria venusta *climbing the walls of Sissinghurst's iconic White Garden*

The restored Elizabethan manor overlooking the garden at Sissinghurst

Rosa complicata—one of many old rose varieties found at Sissinghurst

> "Here the garden rooms are like acts in a play, taking their turn on the stage."

MICHELLE CAIN, FORMER HEAD GARDENER

A GARDEN OF ROOMS

Sissinghurst is based largely on Arts and Crafts garden principles, but the couple created their own unique version of the "garden room" style, blending Harold's perfectionism with Vita's horticultural vim. Garden rooms are filled with distinctive themed arrangements that are striking yet informal in style. Each space has its own particular atmosphere, from the formal cool of the Lime Walk to the hot hues of the South Cottage Garden. The Rondel Rose Garden was Vita's spiritual home. Comically declaring herself "drunk on roses," it was here that she nurtured her passion for old varieties such as Gallicas, Albas, Damasks, and Centifolias. The White Garden, meanwhile, thrills with its soft textures and bridal romance; box- and lavender-edged beds are filled with masses of silver foliage and perennials in their luminous white iterations. The effect is astounding and rarely fails to draw gasps of admiration.

POETRY AND PROSE

Of course, Vita was not only an extraordinary plantswoman; she was also an accomplished author, novelist, poet, and great garden writer. It was in Sissinghurst's Elizabethan Tower, overlooking the garden, that Vita made her writing room. From 1946, she enthralled readers with a weekly gardening column in *The Observer*.

Her sharp wit and authoritative judgments were expressed through honest and uncompromising prose as she shared her horticultural triumphs and disasters at Sissinghurst. She brought her readers along with her on her creative journey, and many came to visit this place that, through Vita's writing and poetry, had so captured their hearts and imaginations. By the late 1950s, the garden was famous.

Vita died at Sissinghurst in 1962, a desolate Harold six years later. This beautiful garden is their lasting legacy, and the spirit of Vita and Harold's original vision undoubtedly lives on.

FOCUS ON

Restoring Vita's Rose Garden

The rose garden was Vita's pride and joy. Over the years she amassed an impressive collection of more than 200 varieties of old roses. Some survived, but many have been lost over time. In 2014, the National Trust began cultivating varieties from Vita's original collection and bringing them back to the rose garden, restoring it to its former glory.

FRANCE · EUROPE

The Hanging Gardens of Marqueyssac

WHERE *24220 Vézac, Périgord* **WHEN** *July and August for candlelit evenings on Thursdays, or fall when the grounds are covered in ivy-leaved cyclamen* **SIZE** *54 acres (22 hectares)*

Clinging to the terraces of a promontory above the Dordogne River, the Hanging Gardens of Marqueyssac are a marvel of green garden making. Visit to be wowed by the clipped perfection of its extraordinary bubbling box parterre.

Marooned on its caterpillar-shaped site, Marqueyssac feels like fairytale domain, meticulously designed to surprise and delight. Walking its pathways is to travel through the varied lands of an epic tale, beginning at the parterre that lies curled like a sleeping dragon. This was exactly what former soldier Julien de Cérval intended in 1861 when he conceived the garden for his newly inherited property, guided by a passion for *Buxus sempervirens* (European boxwood) and the Romantic aesthetic of his time.

TOPIARY MAGIC

Buxus sempervirens is the emblematic plant at Marqueyssac. Obsessively planted by de Cérval, it is everywhere, though most famously seen in the cushioned forms of the Bastion parterre topiary. Here, each plant is unique, hand clipped to perfection, but together they seem to come alive. If you're lucky, you may see the parterre shrouded in mist and bejeweled by a myriad tiny snails, or by candlelight under a midnight sky.

THE PROMONTORY PROMENADE

Each path around the garden, split into three circuits, ends at the Belvedere—a magnificent viewpoint overlooking the river and villages below. The Chapel route, skirting the precipice of the south face, is the most dramatic, dotted with holm oak and resting stations jutting over the valley. Complete the circuit and be met at the château by the real stars of the show: the free-ranging peacocks. Rocky paths, shady arbors, dark tunnels of *Buxus* and secret steps leading to rustic seats contribute to the garden's romanticism tenfold. Indeed, Marqueyssac casts a spell on all who wander through.

150,000

The number of box plants throughout the garden, mostly over one hundred years old, of which 3,500 were newly planted during the restoration of 1996.

Above *Intricate stuccowork detail on La Alhambra's walls*

Left *The inner courtyard framed by surrounding symmetrical architecture, La Alhambra's Court of the Lions*

La Alhambra

WHERE *Granada, Andalusia* WHEN *Spring or fall to avoid the highest temperatures and largest crowds; for an extra-special experience, visit the Nasrid Palace courtyards in the evening* SIZE *32 acres (13 hectares)*

A world of refinement lies behind the walls of "the red one," where the boundaries between buildings and gardens are blurred. Designed on traditional Islamic principles, it is the best surviving example of Moorish and East Mediterranean garden design of the medieval period.

At the Alhambra, you cannot separate the interiors from the exterior spaces. This complex of palaces and gardens is less about plantings; the architecture, rather, is the crowning glory, guiding visitors from beautiful rooms out to sheltered courtyards. It may not be what most people consider a "garden," but many Islamic-style gardens focus more on artistic details than flower borders. Indeed, walls are covered in Arabic inscriptions, tessellated tiles, and pale floral motifs, all finely repeated and reflected in the water of the many pools and fountains.

CAPTIVATING COURTYARDS

The Nasrid Palaces are, without a doubt, the Alhambra's defining image. In and out you walk, following a set route through buildings and gardens that are seamlessly integrated. Rooms give directly onto the courtyards through windows and large open doorways, allowing any cooling breezes to flow right through. Yet, for all the Alhambra's exuberance, the first courtyard,

the Court of the Gilded Room, is a pleasingly spartan space. A scallop-edged water basin bubbles over in the center, evoking a sense of calm. This theme continues in the Court of the Myrtles, where a striking broad pool is lined with straight, symmetrical hedges of myrtle that reflect in the still waters.

It is the Court of the Lions, the most famous, that is saved until last—and what a treat it is. Laid out in a Chahar Bagh, the quintessential Islamic plan based on the gardens of Paradise in the Qur'an, it is divided into quarters by rills arranged in a cross and fed by a central fountain. The seeming simplicity of this four-part layout belies its sophistication. It is believed that the design is based upon geometric principles and calculations using ratios of the lengths and widths of the courtyard and the heights of its columns. These complex measurements are, of course, invisible to the naked eye, but the perfect proportions they create produce a feeling of inherent rightness and a sense of wonder. They add up, somehow, to beauty. →

THE GENERALIFE GARDENS

The Alhambra doesn't keep all its treasures within the complex's confines; lying on the opposite hill, about a 20-minute stroll away, is the Generalife. This area was once the private summer retreat of the emirs, with a smaller, villalike palace and gardens where they would go to escape the heat and take a break from state business. If the main Alhambra site was the rulers' palace city, then the Generalife was like their country estate, with kitchen gardens and orchards laid out on terraces cut into the slopes.

Though originally created in the 13th and 14th centuries, much of today's Generalife was reconstructed more recently in various styles (with the occasional nod to its Moorish past). Indeed, with their mazelike arrangement of tall clipped conifer hedges, arches of roses, and flower beds of bold annuals, the New Gardens—the first sight to gaze upon here—more closely reflect 20th-century European garden ideals.

OLD MEETS NEW

Pebble mosaic paths lead past long rills and spurting fountains—the sound of gushing and gurgling water is everywhere—to yet more courtyards at the Generalife. Only a small portion of the palace still exists, and the original gardens lie some half a yard below what we see now, but the big draw, the Court of the Long Pond, stays somewhat true to what would once have been here. An enclosed, narrow garden, it has a sliver of water at its center and a colonnade along one side with ravishing views across the valley. Dueling jets of water arch over the central channel, which is lined with broad beds of roses, lavender, small orange trees, and herbs. The space marries elements of Islamic garden design with those of the Spanish patio style: brick and terracotta tile paving, pots of evergreens, and climbers spilling from the walls.

The Generalife certainly appeases the desire for greenery. In the Sultana's Garden, also known as the Court of the Cypress, an inward-looking walled garden in the 19th-century Baroque style features a U-shaped canal of water, which wraps around box-edged planting beds. Water features are ubiquitous, and some say the most memorable of all the Generalife's delights is the nearby Water Staircase, leading to the gardens' exit. Ingenious, it features three flights of steps with deep channels scooped out of the banisters, down which clear water gushes.

FOCUS ON

The Nasrids

The Alhambra has had a long and troubled history, but few reliable records remain. What is known, however, is that the Moorish family dynasty known as the Nasrids chose Granada as their royal residence in the 13th century. The palaces and gardens were continually redeveloped by successive Nasrid leaders.

Leaving via a series of parterre-filled terraces and shady walks, lined with tall cypresses and arches of oleander, is to return to the modern world. The scale of the Alhambra is human, the feel is intimate, and this creates a magical atmosphere—one that makes it easy to feel transported back in time, to the era of the Moorish kings who founded this sublime place.

CAREFULLY CURATED

Mythical statues and
cypress trees flanking the
Viottolone, also known
as Viale dei Cipressi or
Cypress Avenue

ITALY · EUROPE

The Boboli Gardens

WHERE *Piazza de' Pitti, Florence* WHEN *April–June, when the grounds are at their prettiest, with spring flowers and fragrant roses* SIZE *111 acres (45 hectares)*

This has everything that one of the most important examples of an Italian Renaissance garden should: crisp geometric lines, carefully clipped hedges, and exuberant grottoes. The Boboli Gardens are a living museum, lovingly curated for centuries in the heart of Florence.

Ranged on a hillside behind the imposing walls of the Pitti Palace, the Boboli Gardens form the largest green space in Florence—a statement of grandeur in both appearance and intention. To stroll along the path from the palace and up to the Fountain of Neptune is to follow in the footsteps of one of the most powerful—and ruthless—families in European history: the Medici. Members of this dynasty were once the effective rulers of Florence, and this was their impeccable private garden.

PLANTED FOR PLEASURE

Work on the garden commenced in 1550, a year after the family took up residence in the Pitti Palace. Eleonora de Toledo, wife of Grand Duke Cosimo I, commissioned the Medici's court artist Niccolò Pericoli (known as Tribolo) to design their haven. His plan was innovative, allowing the garden to act as an extension of the palace, and took its inspiration from the classical gardens of ancient Rome, such as Pliny the Younger's in the upper valley of the Tiber. The arrangement was geometric, with trees and shrubs such as bay laurel, evergreen oaks, and cypresses planted symmetrically. Decorative fountains and a profusion of rare plants, meanwhile, dazzled the senses. Unlike traditional medieval gardens, which were enclosed and inward-looking, this was expansive and embraced distant vistas.

What Tribolo had created was not just a statement of Medici magnificence but a reflection of the Renaissance itself. His design was so inspirational that it influenced the appearance of other royal gardens across Europe, notably Versailles *(p12)*. After his death, the project was taken on by others, with successive palace residents expanding the gardens, shaping them to their taste, and adding the likes of grottoes and statues. →

1819

The date that the great British painter J. M. W. Turner visited the Boboli Gardens and sketched the *Fountain of the Ocean* in the Isolotto. The sketch is now housed in the Tate Britain, London.

A SPECTACULAR STAGE

Courtly pleasure was central to the creation of the gardens, and nothing aided that quite like the amphitheater. Lying to the rear of the palace, this U-shaped space was one of the earliest parts to be laid out and remains its *pièce de résistance*. Ingeniously created from the hollowed-out remains of a stone quarry, it was originally filled with foliage much like a meadow and was known as an "amphitheater of greenery." In later years, however, it was transformed into a grand arena for plays and festivities, with stone walls, statuary, and terraces planted with trees; and in 1790, an Egyptian obelisk—originally erected in Aswan, Egypt, and moved from Rome—was placed in the center to add to the drama.

MONUMENTAL ADORNMENTS

There is, certainly, something theatrical about wandering through Boboli, where inviting paths lead to spectacular grottoes—fashionable adornments of the Italian garden in the 16th century. The most famous of these, tucked away by the side of the palace, is the Grotta del Buontalenti. Inspired by fantastical themes and resembling a cave with rocks, recesses, and stalactites, it exemplifies Mannerist style: exaggerated, artificial, and somewhat florid.

The façade conceals rooms that are finely embellished with shells, roses, and animals and populated with statues, notably *Venus Bathing* by the Flemish sculptor Giambologna.

Though the Grotta del Buontalenti appears merely decorative, its origins were utilitarian. It started life as a reservoir, fed by an aqueduct that carried water from a spring to fill the Boboli's lavish fountains. Alluding to the style of ancient Rome, water was often piped through the mouths of sculptured animals; a fine example is the Bacchus Fountain, where Cosimo I's court jester Pietro Barbino, depicted as the Roman god of wine, sits atop a turtle spurting water from its jaws.

Indeed, water features were integral to any Renaissance garden, and Boboli has a number of them. Making the most striking spectacle is the vast moated garden known as l'Isolotto (Little Island) with Giambologna's statue of Oceanus at its center. It is reached via the Viottolone, a glorious avenue of cypress trees, lined with classical statues. Cool, shady, and decidedly grand, this pathway perfectly evokes the splendor of the days when the Medici walked these paths. They may no longer be exclusively for the elite, but the Boboli Gardens still have a distinct air of aristocratic elegance.

Clockwise from right
Fine views of the Duomo in Florence

The obelisk at the center of the amphitheater

Niches and sculptures adorning the magical Grotta del Buontalenti

TIMELINE OF EVENTS

1550

The Medici commission Niccolò Pericoli, or Tribolo, to design a garden to complement their new residence. He dies soon after work commences, but the task is taken on by others.

1557

Work begins on a large water reservoir, situated close to Cosimo I's orchard. It was hidden by a grand façade and later turned into a decorative grotto, designed by Bernardo Buontalenti.

1774

Construction of the Rococo-style Kaffeehaus begins, the first major addition to the garden by the Hapsburg-Lorraine dynasty who succeeded the Medici. It was a place for the court to enjoy a hot chocolate on walks.

1790

The Egyptian obelisk is erected in the amphitheater. Dedicated to Ramesses II, it was taken to Rome in the 1st century AD, then later transferred to the Villa Medici. The journey from Rome to Florence took four months.

Dumbarton Oaks

W H E R E *1703 32nd Street NW, Washington, DC* **W H E N** *Spring, when the early flowering trees blossom and the flowers bloom, creating a pretty spectacle* **S I Z E** *16 acres (6 hectares)*

Nothing is left to chance at Dumbarton Oaks, where kindred spirits Mildred Bliss and Beatrix Farrand planned every bench, border, plant, and urn over three decades. Often described as a series of surprises, Dumbarton Oaks is a testament to precise planning and passion.

When art collector Mildred Bliss and her husband, Robert, purchased their ideal country house in 1920, their main desire was to create superb gardens. A year later, Mildred had commissioned the famed landscape gardener Beatrix Farrand to help them achieve this. The Blisses traveled a lot (Robert worked in the US Foreign Service), and so much of the communication between Mildred and Farrand was via detailed letters. The two grew close, calling themselves "gardening twins," and it is their passionate planning over 30 years that makes Dumbarton Oaks such an admirable feat.

PRESERVED GROUNDS

Even when the grounds were gifted to Harvard University in 1941 to create a research institute, the women still continued shaping the landscape. Beatrix even wrote a book to aid the future upkeep of the gardens, explaining the reasons behind her designs and how to care for the plants.

Nearly a century later, Farrand and Mildred's work remains intact. Behind the Federal-style house atop a hill, the Orangery is a gateway

into a series of themed garden "rooms" and intricate tiers. Those closest to the house are the most formal, mainly in the classical European style. The further one moves downhill, the more informal the gardens become, transitioning to a more naturalistic and modern American style. Each discrete room has multiple access points yet manages to feel enclosed and private, inviting the contemplation of a unique vista or feature. The multiple benches placed regularly in the landscape are no coincidence—this is not a garden to be rushed through.

FOCUS ON

Ornaments

The numerous statues and urns placed in the landscape were first mocked up in clay and brought to the location so they could be approved by Mildred, before they were hand-carved in stone.

Clockwise from right
*Colorful flowers
contained in beds*

*Pink plum trees lining
a path through the
Kitchen Gardens*

*An elegant urn
gracing the Urn Terrace*

IF YOU LIKE THIS

Nymans

UK · EUROPE

Starting in the late 19th century and continuing through the 20th century, three generations of the Messel family—the women, in particular—played a pivotal role in shaping this garden in West Sussex. The rose garden is a highlight, created by Maud Messel in the 1920s and filled with scented plants from her gardening friends.

MINDFUL SPACES

The concept of biophilia insists that humans have an innate need to connect with the natural world—no surprise, given how much being enveloped in nature boosts our well-being. It might be the very act of touching the soil when gardening that brings us focus, or witnessing the seasons change on a daily walk that reinvigorates our spirit. Most gardens by definition are relaxing spaces, but when you're in awe at the status-driven opulence of Versailles, taking a quiet moment may not be your first reaction. Mindful gardens, on the other hand, soothe the mind and spirit at every turn.

CONTEMPLATIVE DESIGNS

Gardens are certainly somewhere to have a good think. Charles Jencks used his garden to work through scientific theories on the universe, while others crafted private refuges that would inspire them to create art or music. On a deeper level, gardens can awaken spirituality, whether it's a tranquil space that encourages religious prayer or a vast landscape that aids connection with an indigenous horticultural past.

If any type of garden has exerted a strong influence on the creation of contemplative spaces, it's the Japanese garden. Though not one single style (there are myriad components behind each one), Japanese gardens are typically all cherished for their spiritual and philosophical ideas. As such, symbolism is heavy—water is regarded as purifying, plantings tend to be subtle, and winding paths aid concentration, for starters. Gardeners in the West have turned to the Japanese style for inspiration in many ways, but it's not always a case of imitating them; rather, it's about encapsulating the spirit of such restrained landscapes.

HELPING WELL-BEING

Creating a garden can in itself be just as thought-provoking and calming as visiting one. There's perhaps nothing more soothing than focusing on rewilding a space, deciding which color combinations to plant, or the very act of sowing seeds. Having something to nurture can be consoling, as Wendy Whiteley found when she was grieving, or Elsie Reford when an operation forced her to find a new hobby. The physical act of moving the earth can give us purpose and teach us the patience to wait for something to grow and blossom.

Gardens provide us with a space to create and contemplate. Whether it's visiting an existing haven or making it ourselves, there's nothing like connecting with nature.

RIKUGIEN
JAPAN

BLOEDEL RESERVE
US

LIMAHULI GARDEN AND PRESERVE
US

RYŌAN-JI
JAPAN

KATSURA RIKYŪ IMPERIAL VILLA
JAPAN

MONET'S GARDENS AT GIVERNY
FRANCE

THE BAHA'Í GARDENS
ISRAEL

THE GARDEN OF COSMIC SPECULATION
UK

WENDY'S SECRET GARDEN
AUSTRALIA

GIARDINI LA MORTELLA
ITALY

JARDINS DE MÉTIS
CANADA

SPIRITED GARDEN
SOUTH KOREA

Rikugien

WHERE *6-16-3 Hon'komagome, Bunkyō Ward, Tokyo* **WHEN** *Seasonal highlights include flowering cherries (late March), azaleas (mid-April to early May, then late May to early June) and fall leaf color (mid-November to early December)* **SIZE** *25 acres (10 hectares)*

Tucked among the bustling streets of Tokyo, this gracious garden points to literature as its main inspiration. Featuring a series of symbolic landscapes designed to delight, Rikugien captures the transient beauty of the seasons that is celebrated in classical Japanese poetry.

The central highlight of this peaceful garden is an area of open lawn dominated by a shimmering lake. From there, a path gives way to a shadow of overhanging trees, where glossy dark-green foliage creates the illusion of a mountain forest; further along, a deciduous woodland beckons as sunlight flickers down through the leaves above and bamboo grasses rustle beneath. Rikugien is, after all, an exquisite Japanese *kaiyū-shiki* ("stroll" garden), where winding paths reveal unexpected views to both surprise and delight.

Designed to be admired from every angle, stroll gardens became popular with the nobility during the Edo Period (1603–1868). These places of pleasure and enjoyment often reproduced small versions of famous landscapes or scenes from literature, and Rikugien is no different. Yoshiyasu Yanagisawa, the samurai nobleman who built Rikugien in the 17th century, had a deep love for Japanese poetry, and his garden recreates landscapes from famous *waka* (poems).

Variety within the garden is produced not only by the ever-changing scenery but also by the cycle of the seasons. Glorious azaleas bloom and fade in the balmy air of spring. Japanese maples begin to shimmer in late November, their golden glow lasting all too briefly. Mist settles over the lake in the depth of winter. Everything is constantly changing, offering opportunities for contemplation along with precious moments of discovery.

TRY IT AT HOME

Concealment

Japanese gardens use the art of partial concealment to tickle the curiosity of visitors and to stir their imagination. Consider leaving features such as waterfalls and stone lanterns partly veiled behind foliage to create surprise.

IF YOU LIKE THIS

Cowra Japanese Garden

AUSTRALIA ·
AUSTRALASIA

Under the wide skies of New South Wales, this Japanese-style stroll garden, with its large pond and expansive vistas, inspires calm. Native flora blends in seamlessly with traditional Japanese garden plants.

Anderson Japanese Gardens

USA · NORTH AMERICA

Garden designer Hōichi Kurisu reinterprets the concept of the Japanese stroll garden here, near Chicago, to highlight the tranquillity of North American forest and lake landscapes and celebrate the rhythm of the seasons.

Bloedel Reserve

WHERE *7571 NE Dolphin Drive, Bainbridge Island, Washington*
WHEN *November to January, when winter bloomers are on display* **SIZE** *150 acres*

Framed by the sparkling waters of Puget Sound, Bloedel Reserve is the epitome of a garden perfectly balanced with nature. It changes with the seasons, but the Bloedel vision, to show how restorative nature can be, delivers every time.

The Sand and Stone Garden in the Bloedel Reserve's award-winning Japanese Garden

Just a short ferry ride from downtown Seattle, on Bainbridge Island, sits the Bloedel Reserve, a stunning mix of natural woodlands, open meadows, and painstakingly manicured landscaped gardens. It's an Eden-like paradise, a green retreat with serene trails that take the visitor past sweeping vistas, marshlands, and forests, and wildlife habitats teeming with birdlife. Clean, fresh, earthy notes fill the air with a hint of ocean breeze on the outer trails. It's an alluring, multisensory experience—a study in nature that promises vibrant colors, distinctive textures, bold shapes, and an array of scents.

AHEAD OF HIS TIME

"Nature can do without man, but man cannot do without nature." Such was the belief of the reserve's founder, Prentice Bloedel. Bloedel was ahead of his time when he created this natural refuge just a stone's throw from the city. He had a deep appreciation and understanding of the therapeutic powers of nature, funding early research into the psychological benefits of spending time in a natural environment.

He and his wife, Virginia, transformed the large wooded tract they purchased in 1951 with therapeutic gardens, soothing pools, and verdant lawns. Their aim was to capture the subtlety, tranquility, and simplicity of the Japanese garden in their Western expression of it. To this day, the gardens and reserve attract visitors from the world over who come here in search of calm and solace.

BOTANICAL BEAUTY

Around 2 miles (3 km) of spongy trails guide visitors through the reserve and its 23 distinct landscapes. The trail begins in a meadow of ornamental grasses, taking visitors past the Buxton Bird Marsh and Meadow where nesting birds and dragonflies reside. →

In spring, 50 different native wildflowers and 50,000 bulbs planted in the adjacent meadow bloom in vibrant succession, attracting pollinators and other insects. Next comes an enchanting forested area, where a boardwalk zigzags across wetlands home to frogs, carnivorous plants, and other aquatic flora and fauna. Past the Bloedels' former residence, designed in the 18th-century French tradition, is the Japanese garden and the largest public moss garden in the US, its velvetlike carpet comprising over 40 species of moss and lichen.

The exquisitely rendered Japanese garden was twice named one of the top 10 Japanese gardens in the US by the *Journal of Japanese Gardening*. While gazing out over the garden from the Japanese Guest House, it's not difficult to see why. This is a place of peaceful contemplation. Asian pines grace the area,

1970

The year that the Bloedels gifted their reserve to the University of Washington, after fearing that their estate would be heavily altered or even destructed after their death. They trusted the university, given its reputation in horticulture and forestry.

including Japanese black pine, Japanese white pine, and Japanese red pine, all cloud pruned in the traditional Japanese style. The Japanese Sand and Stone Garden portrays islands surrounded by sea, its simplicity evoking a sense of peace and serenity.

COLORS AND TEXTURES

Prentice Bloedel was color-blind, so he was more interested in textures and varying shades of green than colorful flowers, but that didn't stop him from planting an array of vibrant blooms throughout the reserve. This is best seen in the flowering meadows, as well as the woodland gardens, where swathes of trout lily *(Erythronium)* and candelabra primroses—one of Virginia Bloedel's favorite flowers—bloom each spring. Glorious blooms await in the Rhododendron Glen and along the Camellia and Orchid trails, too. Here, hardy cyclamen produce white to pink flowers in late summer and early fall, pretty hellebores bloom in winter and striking navelwort lines the paths in spring.

Whatever the season, Bloedel Reserve's natural beauty will hold you spellbound. And don't let the size of the reserve deter you. The walks are relaxing and easy, and there are numerous benches along the way to rest. Take time out of your busy schedule to recharge your batteries. You'll thank nature for it.

Clockwise from top left

Silver birch rising from the shrubs on the Birch Trail

Visitors exploring the Rhododendron Glen in bloom

The Bloedels' former residence overlooking the main lake

The Japanese Guest House deck

Limahuli Garden and Preserve

WHERE *5-8291 Kuhio Hwy, Ha'ena, Kaua'i, Hawaii* **WHEN** *Hawaii's islands enjoy warm temperatures and lower rainfall March–September; early morning is best to beat the crowds and enjoy the gardens in peace* **SIZE** *Garden: 17 acres (6.9 hectares); preserve: 985 acres (399 hectares)*

Tucked away in one of the world's most biodiverse environments, the Limahuli Garden and Preserve unveils the natural landscape that Hawaii's first people encountered, the flora they introduced, and the revival of their sustainable cultivation practices.

After navigating the cliff-hugging Kuhio Highway nearly to its end, you arrive at the entrance to the Limahuli Garden and Preserve, shielded within the base of a high mountain ridge known as Makana. Still dewy after the morning's rain, the grounds are rich in vivid greens with flashes of red, orange, and yellow. A small wooden sign marks the start of the garden trail, a paved footpath that weaves upward through lush vegetation before descending back down again to conclude a 0.6-mile (1 km) loop.

The path begins by intersecting several terraces built into the slope of the valley, some flush with the water-loving *kalo* (taro) plants. The brown, lichen-covered lava rocks used to build the terraces were initially laid here some thousand years earlier by Hawaii's first settlers. Crossing the vast Pacific Ocean on canoes from Polynesia, these skilled seafarers brought with them a selection of plants such as coconut palm, banana, and sugar cane. Aptly named "canoe plants," and grown here in Limahuli's

first section of the garden, they would sustain the settlers' new life on Kaua'i, and subsequently on the rest of the Hawaiian Islands.

NEW ARRIVALS

It wasn't just a handful of seedlings that came with early settlers but a profound respect for their new terra firma—one that Limahuli hopes to reforge with biocultural conservation. This approach to preserving plant species honors the relationship between nature and humanity, and visitors are encouraged to be mindful of the cultural and historical significance of plants with every step they take through the garden. →

250

The number of native Hawaiian plants and birds within Limahuli Garden and Preserve, many of which are either rare or near the brink of extinction.

Left *Visitor exploring Limahuli Garden*

Next page *A pathway cutting through dense layers of vegetation*

IF YOU LIKE THIS

Madeira Botanical Garden

PORTUGAL · EUROPE

Native Madeiran plants, many of which are rare or extinct in the wild, are safeguarded here.

First Nations Garden

CANADA · NORTH AMERICA

This Montreal garden is full of flora that are culturally significant to Quebec and its First Nations and Inuit peoples.

Crossing over several wooden boardwalks, the path continues upward to the second section of the garden, which represents the plant species introduced to the Hawaiian Islands over the last two centuries. Plantation workers arriving from Asia and European missionaries brought with them a variety of species, many of them ornamental and noted for their delightful fragrance or enchanting beauty. Here, the neon-orange spikes of bird-of-paradise poke out from behind a tangle of mango and papaya tree limbs, vying for space with heliconia, orchids, and pineapples, a former crop industry of Hawaii. Many of these species became iconic to Hawaii, despite not being native.

NURTURING NATIVE PLANTS

Limahuli's intention is to celebrate not only plants introduced here but endemic species, too. This hasn't been an easy task, however. Though Kaua'i is brimming with lush vegetation, most of the greenery on the island is not indigenous, since many native species have gone—or are going—extinct. The Native Forest Walk, next along the path, instead recreates an authentic mesic forest of native species, reflecting how Hawaii's first people would have encountered it all those centuries ago.

Acacia koa trees dappled with brown seed pods and hala trees with lengthy prop roots are both part of this recreation. Plants of all sizes thrive in a spacious setting with soft streaks of

sunlight filtering in, although many placards are inscribed with words like "endangered," "extinct," or "Hawaiian name lost"—testament to how few native species are left on the island. Few are flowering plants, with some exceptions, such as the yellow *Hibiscus brackenridgei*, Hawaii's state flower, and the *Metrosideros polymorpha*, or 'ōhi'a lehua, one of Hawaii's best-loved trees.

Limahuli Stream flowing through the garden and irrigating the land

REFLECTION AND INSPIRATION

As the path leads back down to the visitor center, one last stop at a productive micro-garden demonstrates how Kaua'i's residents can restore a balanced native landscape in their own backyard. Limahuli no doubt leaves you in awe of the beauty of Kaua'i and its varied plant life, native or not. But, by looking to the past, the garden also invokes reflection and a sense of shared responsibility for the ecological future of our planet.

Ryōan-ji

WHERE *13 Ryōanji Goryō-no-shita-chō, Ukyō Ward, Kyoto* WHEN *Year round, though cherries flower from late March to early April* SIZE *0.06 acres (0.02 hectares)*

In this small enclosed garden at Ryōan-ji, a Zen Buddhist temple in Japan's ancient capital of Kyoto, stones and gravel take center stage instead of plants. The result is a challenge to every preconception about what defines a garden.

To mention Ryōan-ji, the temple founded in the middle of the 15th century, is to speak of its iconic stone garden. Located on the south side of the *hōjō* (abbot's hall), the Ryōan-ji stone garden comprises 15 carefully chosen stones, grouped roughly into five clusters, set in raked gravel. Nature has been pared down here to its bare bones. Indeed, this is not a garden that offers instant visions of grandeur or sublimity. At first glance, the rectangular garden, surrounded on three sides by walls fissured by time, seems unexpectedly modest. The abbot's hall, meanwhile—never intended to welcome so many visitors at once—can get packed and noisy. But wait. When the crowds drift off, you will have a moment all to yourself.

IN THE MOMENT

Stylistically, Ryōan-ji belongs to the Japanese tradition of the *karesansui* ("dry landscape") garden, in which gravel is used to represent water—a river, for example, or the sea. Being "dry" does not imply that such gardens are arid. Lush moss, trees, and evergreen shrubs are often used to represent a verdant shoreline. The minimalist design of Ryōan-ji has inspired many interpretations; that it symbolizes the harmony of the universe, or the stones represent a tiger helping her cubs cross a river, an image of Buddha's mercy. Still, it defies definitive answers because its history is so obscure. Who created this garden, when or why is unknown.

Certainly Ryōan-ji confronts us with a desire to "make sense" of our surroundings, yet Buddhism teaches the dangers of mistaking thoughts for reality itself. It can be a relief to stop rationalizing and open yourself up to the sensations of the garden—the quality of the light, the feeling of space, the solidity of the stones, the shadows cast by the many trees growing on the other side of the wall. Be in the moment and immerse yourself in the shapes, sounds, and textures of this garden—a design of subtle, artistic sophistication.

Clockwise from right
Kyōyōchi Pond in the temple grounds

Gravel symbolizing a calm ocean, and stones representing distant rocky islands

Lush greenery surrounding the temple

IF YOU LIKE THIS

Yū-sui-en Japanese Garden, Erholungspark Marzahn

GERMANY · EUROPE

This *karesansui* garden was created in Berlin in 2003 by the contemporary Japanese garden designer Shunmyō Masuno. As a Zen Buddhist monk, Masuno considers designing gardens to be part of, as well as an expression of, his ascetic spiritual discipline.

Katsura Rikyū Imperial Villa

WHERE *Katsura-misono, Ukyō Ward, Kyoto* **WHEN** *Late April and into early May, when the scarlet azalea* Rhododendron obtusum *comes into flower* **SIZE** *14 acres (6 hectares)*

Created by imperial princes in the 17th century, Katsura Rikyū is an elegant landscape garden, with rustic teahouses dotted amid woodland and surrounding a central lake. It effortlessly blends the intimacy of a tea garden with sweeping panoramic scenery.

A product of the cultural milieu of its period, Katsura was built as a country retreat by its owner, the imperial prince Hachijō-no-miya Toshihito (1579–1629). The garden, with its lake, hills, pavilions, and bridges, was designed to provide a succession of scenic views for the pleasure of the prince's guests as they walked along the paths or took a boat out onto the lake, all before enjoying a tea ceremony. Toshihito's son, Hachijō-no-miya Toshitada (1619–1662) later built upon the exquisite achievements of his father, enhancing the scope of the garden.

MAKING CHANGES

Toshitada shared his father's taste for simplicity and graceful lines. He enlarged the garden, extending the southern end of the lake, making its shoreline more varied and creating new views. Katsura's strength certainly lies in the manner in which its paths and stepping stones control the visitor's line of sight, resulting in a series of ingeniously planned vistas. For example, the eye is led progressively from a stone lantern in the foreground, across the water, to an arched bridge in the middle distance, and then further on into the far distance, where there might be a glimpse of a teahouse or of the elegant villa buildings. This use of perspective gives the garden a feeling of expansiveness that belies its actual size. →

Looking out to the Shōkin-tei teahouse from Prince Toshitada's roji-garden path.

TRY IT AT HOME

Stone Features

When first setting up a stone lantern or a stone water basin in your garden, plant a couple of ferns or evergreen perennials such as *Liriope muscari* around their base to help make them look settled in and a part of your landscape.

THE TEA CEREMONY

Teahouses form an integral part of this garden's magnificent landscape. While Toshihito's tea rooms opened out onto views of the garden, his son also took an interest in the *roji*-style tea garden. This style emerged late in the 16th century with the development of the *wabi*-style tea ceremony, which aimed to refine the ceremony down to its key elements: preparing a bowl of tea for guests.

Wabi-style tea ceremonies were often held in confined, rustic tea rooms, modeled after an idealized image of a hermit's forest retreat. The *roji*-style gardens leading to such tea rooms were designed to suggest woodland, and passing through them represented the idea of seeking out an ascetic's humble cottage. Just as the *wabi*-style tea ceremony emphasized the present, the *roji*-style tea garden prepared guests for the upcoming ceremony, taking them out of the everyday world.

Various features of the *roji* garden, which does not need to be large, are designed to help focus the mind on the present moment. Walking gracefully along stepping stones requires calm concentration. The act of crouching beside a small stone water basin to purify your hands before the ceremony emphasizes the significance of what you are doing. Toshitada's choice of stepping stones and stone basins, along with their layout, exemplifies this principle.

EXPANSIVE VIEWS

Nonetheless, Toshitada lived at a time of great creative flux, and his tea garden does not strictly fit latter-day conventions of the *roji*-style garden. The path leading from the waiting arbor to the *wabi*-style tea room passes along the edge of the garden lake, where there are superb views to be had. It could be argued that these views constitute a distraction, but the prince pursued his own ideas of beauty. One such view, of islands connected with low stone bridges, was created by Toshitada's father to mirror his favorite scenic landscape: Ama-no-hashidate, a pine-covered spit of land that stretches across a bay on Japan's coast. Its symbolic representation here is a marvelous example of the Japanese art of miniaturization, with the lake standing for the sea. Far from treating it as a distraction, Toshitada made this view the highlight of his *roji*-style tea garden.

CALM JOYFULNESS

Walking along the *roji* path, past the rustic waiting arbor, the discreet stone lanterns and basins, is to leave the modern world behind. While the brisk obligatory tour nowadays allows little time for quiet contemplation, focusing on each moment lets you appreciate the beauty of Katsura Rikyū's entire garden and its calming effect.

Top *A view across the lake from inside the Geppa-rō teahouse*

Bottom *Intricate stone pavement leading from an arched bridge to the main villa buildings*

IF YOU LIKE THIS

Shūgaku-in Rikyū Imperial Villa

JAPAN • ASIA

In the 1650s, the former emperor Go-mizuno'o created his own rural retreat, comprised of a series of intimate landscaped gardens built along the slope of a hill on the outskirts of Kyoto. At the uppermost garden, panoramic views of the lake await, the surrounding countryside with its rice fields, and Kyoto itself.

Monet's Gardens at Giverny

WHERE *84 Rue Claude Monet, Giverny, Normandy* WHEN *The garden looks great throughout its open season (April 1 to November 1), but for a chance to beat the crowds, visit in April or October and arrive early in the day* SIZE *8.6 acres (3.5 hectares)*

Claude Monet described Giverny as his greatest work of art, but this carefully orchestrated paradise was also his most enduring inspiration. Today, the garden beautifully reflects the artist's love of flowers and nature, and his lifelong obsession with color, pattern, and light.

There's something special about Giverny, a place alive with the spirit of the man who called it home for so many years. Monet moved to Giverny with his family in 1883, attracted by the area's bucolic charm—its flower meadows and rolling fields, pretty orchards and quivering poplars—and, unsurprisingly, its luminosity. Here in the countryside of the Seine valley, a number of Impressionist artists found inspiration for their work, not least Monet, who created hundreds of his signature light-suffused paintings in his new surroundings.

Certainly Giverny proved a strong influence on Monet's work, providing an ever-shifting canvas of plants to nourish his creativity. But it was also a dazzling work of horticultural art in itself. You may visit to see Monet's paintings in three dimensions, but the gardens themselves will soon have you captivated, enveloping you in their varying moods—at times bursting with color and fragrance, at others subdued and reflective, but always beguiling.

CLOS NORMAND

Immediately intimate, the Clos Normand, the first of Monet's two gardens, is an ever-shifting kaleidoscope of blooms. Spring here means bulbs aplenty. Narcissi, daffodils, crown imperials, and tulips emerge from underplantings of purple forget-me-nots and pansies, offset by cheerful mounds of aubretia. →

TRY IT AT HOME

A Monet Container

Add a *soupçon* of Giverny's French country charm to your garden by growing candy-pink tulips underplanted with a cloud of forget-me-nots. The style lends itself to containers, and you can experiment with the tulip colors for a bolder effect.

Radiant plantings adorning the sweeping arches of Monet's beloved Clos Normand

Clockwise from top

*Pink and green hues
of Monet's house*

*Bright florals lining the
path through the Clos
Normand to the
Maison du Pressoir*

*Gladioli protruding from
a thick underplanting*

Irises takes center stage for a few brief weeks in May, when the garden becomes an exquisite assortment of purples and golds. Throughout the summer, roses emerge. Together with the peonies, they fill the air with their sweet perfume. Late in the summer, the garden's wow factor reaches its zenith with a dazzling show of dahlias, hollyhocks, and sunflowers. They bloom well into the fall, when they are joined by clouds of Michaelmas daisies set against the golden glow of turning leaves.

The Clos Normand reflects Monet's passion for color and nature at its most exuberant. He was constantly adding new plants, forever playing with color schemes. Monet's paintings were largely composed of daubs of primary colors, and his planting was equally vibrant. His colors were pure, rarely tonally watered down. He combined blues with reds and yellows with purples, planting hot color schemes facing west to amplify their glow in the setting sun and placing his blue bearded irises in the half shade to bring out their jewel-like luminescence.

PRETTY IN PINK

Overlooking the Clos Normand is Monet's house, a pretty pink farmhouse known as the Maison du Pressoir. It was previously a cider

farm; Monet gradually replaced the old apple trees with flowering Japanese cherries and apricots. He painted the windows and shutters green to reflect the natural environment. Throughout the gardens, benches, plant supports, and bridges sport the same color, a clever leitmotif to link the gardens together.

1896

The year Monet started painting his famous water lilies. He became obsessed with capturing what he called these "landscapes of water," working on them until his death 30 years later. He produced at least 250 paintings on this subject.

To further enhance this connection, he grew a Virginia creeper against the walls of the house and planted climbing roses on the veranda. Meanwhile, nearby beds were punctuated with a beautiful display of weeping standard roses and decorative rose arches. He created a vision in pink and green, the garden cleverly echoing the colors of the house, and the house perfectly blending with the beauty of the garden. →

THE WATER GARDEN

Monet's beloved water garden is, undoubtedly, Giverny's defining image. The now iconic part of the garden started as a passion project of Monet's, something that thrilled and excited him in its creation. In 1893, 10 years after moving to Giverny, Monet acquired a marshy plot of land across the road from his house. He planned to divert the nearby river and create a water garden adorned with aquatic plants. Slowly, he realized his dream.

FOCUS ON

A Point to Prove

Some locals were wary of Monet's plans and were concerned that the water garden would be filled with contaminating plants. Indignant, Monet wrote a letter to the regional prefect, insisting that it was to be a place of leisure and to provide a subject for painting. To Monet, poisoning the water was out of the question.

Over the following years, he dug out a pond, edged it with sinuous paths, crossed it with bridges, and planted acers, water-loving irises, bamboos, tree peonies, and wisteria. Compared to the open and sunny Clos Normand, the shaded water garden is serene and subdued. To reach it, you must walk through a small tunnel that transports you into a world where weeping willows drape across the water's edge and lilies glide atop its glassy surface. Every turn in the water garden brings with it a new vista that recalls one of Monet's Impressionist paintings—including, of course, the famous view of the bridge reaching across the water.

Monet's choice of plants was heavily inspired by his love of Japanese art. A number of specimens came directly from Japan as gifts, including tree peonies and lilies from Princess Matsukata and her art collector husband, Kōjirō. Monet's planting technique was also influenced by the Japanese aesthetic, in particular its rejection of traditional perspective and its emphasis on the decorative. Here in the water garden and in the paintings it inspired, water, land, and sky merge into one, bound together by an all-enveloping light. Much like Japanese stroll gardens, the paths and bridges of the Water Garden invite you to slow down and take in the moment.

What Monet yearned for was to capture what he called "instantaneity"—snapshots of moments in time. The constant play of shadow and light, the changing colors and reflections—it was all so mesmerizing to him. He would walk around his garden three or four times a day in awe at the beauty of nature. Sometimes, for full immersion, he would even paint from his boat. You may not be able to join him on the water, but as you stand on one of the many bridges to admire the scenery, you may feel something of the spell it cast on the artist. At the very least, you will want to take a turn around the garden one more time.

Top
Wisteria draped over a bridge in the water garden

Bottom
Water lilies floating on the water's surface

TIMELINE OF EVENTS

1883

Monet and his family settle at Giverny.

1893

Monet acquires land across the road and starts creating his water garden.

1926

Aged 86, Monet dies at Giverny. His son Michel inherits the estate but never lives there. Monet's stepdaughter Blanche looks after it until her death in 1947, after which it goes into decline.

1977

The house and gardens at Giverny undergo extensive restorations under the curatorship of Gérald van der Kemp.

1980

The Fondation Claude Monet is established and Giverny opens to the public in September.

The Baha'í Gardens

WHERE *61 Yefe Nof Street, Haifa* **WHEN** *Year round, but the weather is most comfortable in spring and fall* **SIZE** *50 acres (20 hectares)*

The Baha'í Gardens are a work of art and an oasis of tranquility built to celebrate the Baha'í faith. The terraced hillside gardens attract a million visitors annually, including many Baha'í pilgrims and others drawn by the uplifting atmosphere that this stunning location inspires.

The Baha'í Gardens roll down the hillside of Mount Carmel, blending the formality and symmetry of traditional Persian paradise gardens with local flora and Western design. The gardens have an emotional, spiritual, and functional role—stimulating the senses through nature and beauty, encouraging prayer through their tranquility, and connecting the buildings that comprise the headquarters of the Baha'í faith.

A SPIRITUAL CONNECTION

This is a holy site, and a visit requires modest dress and hushed respect. Except during guided tours, visitors are restricted to the upper balcony section only. Yet even here, the serenity and spiritual significance of the location, along with stunning views of the Mediterranean below, all stimulate soulful contemplation.

The grand central staircase features a total of 19 terraces, each one designed in the neo-classical European style. On the 10th terrace is the gold-domed shrine with the tomb of the Bab, one of the central figures of the Baha'í faith. The Bab prophesied the coming of a

"Promised One" who would found a new universal religion. The other 18 terraces symbolize each one of his 18 disciples.

STRIKING A BALANCE

The staircase comprises some 1,500 steps and is lined with stone balustrades and well-trimmed cypresses, pristine lawns, and formal flower beds in carefully designed circular and star-shaped geometric precision. Diligent gardeners abound, carefully nurturing and busily grooming. There are nearly 500 plant species here, most of which are native to the Eastern Mediterranean and carefully selected to minimize the need for watering, with seasonal flowers adding splashes of contrasting color to the green of the grass and trees. True to the Islamic style, however, there is emphasis on shade and water, with ornate fountains, channels, and ponds all featuring prominently.

The weaving of Eastern and Western garden design is, of course, no accident. The use of multiple styles is used intentionally, illustrative of the intended universalism of the Baha'í faith.

Clockwise from right

The terraces of the Baha'i Gardens cascading down the hillside toward the sea

Panoramic views over Haifa and the coast from the uppermost terrace

Purple Agapanthus flowers in bloom

IF YOU LIKE THIS

Bagh-e Fin

IRAN · MIDDLE EAST

Bagh-e Fin in Kashan is a delight of ancient trees, pools and fountains fed by a natural spring, all arranged in the classic formality and symmetry typical of Persian garden design. Completed in 1590, Bagh-e Fin is the oldest existing garden in Iran, and it was a strong influence on the design of the Baha'i Gardens.

The Garden of Cosmic Speculation

WHERE *Portrack House, Holywood, Dumfries, Scotland* **WHEN** *Once a year in May as part of Scotland's Gardens Scheme* **SIZE** *30 acres (12 hectares)*

Based on the idea of gardens as allegories, the imaginative Garden of Cosmic Speculation was one man's vision to celebrate and represent scientific theories. The sculptures and landforms that erupt in this pastoral setting certainly open the minds of those lucky enough to visit.

The southwest of Scotland is a landscape of gently rolling hills and wooded valleys, where time seems to move at a slower pace. But near the tiny hamlet of Holywood lies a wrinkle in the fabric of this bucolic setting: a surreal garden inspired by science and mathematics, where strange landforms, serpentine lakes, and bridges twist in the air before plunging beneath the soil. Rare not just in its appearance, the Garden of Cosmic Speculation is open only once a year, so visiting it is as extraordinary a treat as the landscape itself.

MEANINGFUL METAPHORS

Creating a garden as unique as this—its water staircases tumbling in perilous steps down steep hillsides, and terraces seemingly sucked underground by a hidden force—takes great curiosity, imagination, and intellect. And that's exactly what architect Charles Jencks and garden designer Maggie Keswick brought to the project when they started its build. In 1988, the couple set out to turn a boggy field on Keswick's

family's estate into a swimming pond for their children. Yet as the earth was excavated and the spoil mounds grew, Jencks began to see their possibilities and set out to invent a new type of landform architecture. This was a time when Jencks's own interest in new discoveries in cosmic science was growing rapidly. To Jencks, a garden was a miniature representation of the universe, a natural place to celebrate the very nature of existence. The landscape soon became a canvas for symbolic exploration.

Allegorical gardens are not new. As early as 550 BCE, Cyrus the Great was laying out his garden at Pasargadae, on the Murghab plain, along what would become known as the Persian "Paradise" tradition, with its rills representing the rivers that flowed out of Edefn. In the Middle Ages, the *hortus conclusus*, or enclosed garden, was rich in Christian significance. Though this level of symbolism seemed to cease in later centuries, with gardens created for pleasure or beauty, the Garden of Cosmic Speculation is a welcome return to such traditions. →

Top *DNA sculptures rising from the green landscape*

Bottom *The Snake Mound and the Snail beautifully sculpted into the earth*

IF YOU LIKE THIS

Landform Udea

UK · EUROPE

Swirling around the Scottish National Gallery of Modern Art in Edinburgh is Charles Jencks's sculptural response to chaos theory.

The Tarot Garden

ITALY · EUROPE

Nestled in the Maremma countryside, Niki de Saint Phalle's garden of strange, grotesque, and curvaceous sculptures, many covered in mirrored shards, is based on the occult.

"When you design a garden, it raises basic questions. What is nature, how do we fit into it, and how should we shape it where we can, both physically and visually?"

CHARLES JENCKS

PLAYING WITH PERCEPTIONS

Over the years, the couple met with physicists and cosmic scientists to come up with a design that merged science, art, and nature. They began to give physical shape to fundamental scientific ideas and metaphors—some as old as time, and some that reflected the rush of new discoveries that were coming thick and fast at the beginning of the 21st century.

Every gate, fence, wall, and paving stone in the garden—made up of five areas—represents a key discovery about the origins of the universe and the life that it sustains. The mound of earth that came from digging the pool, an area now known as the Snail Mound, was sculpted into a double helix to represent the form of DNA. Throughout the landscape, more sculptures of this iconic symbol of life are dotted around. Where the land drops behind their house, Jencks created the Universe Cascade. Here, every section portrays a different era of existence, from the beginning of time through the emergence of the first stars to the present day. Beyond the house, the Black Hole Terrace, made up of twisting forms in the grass, represents the distortion of time and space. Even the crestings on the roof of the greenhouses are formed from equations discovered by Lagrange, Schrodinger and other physicists that help disentangle the complexities of existence.

SPACE FOR RUMINATION

Visiting this otherworldly, sprawling space is to experience laughter and disbelief, confusion and admiration, deep thought and distraction all at once. Of course, the Garden of Cosmic Speculation is not a garden in the traditional sense. Familiar garden features appear to morph into something strange, unexpected elements emerge from the ground, paths lead to unsettling glades, and always there is the feeling that the visitor is in a shifting space.

FOCUS ON

Maggie's Centers

Maggie Keswick Jencks's instinctive understanding of nature was an integral part of the development of the Garden of Cosmic Speculation. When diagnosed with terminal cancer, she poured her energies into creating a network of cancer caring centers set in distinctive buildings, all with inspirational gardens.

Ultimately, though, this is a private garden that was never intended for visitors. Wandering around it on the one day a year that it opens is to get a special insight into the minds and interests of its creators, and—like them—to contemplate the unseen forces that are always at work around us. Being here is not, however, to be pressured into untangling the theories represented beneath your feet or to feel overwhelmed by the intellectual complexities that are hinted at in the land. Simply basking in the solitude and the impeccably crafted landforms is enough to make you appreciate your existence in this universe.

Wendy's Secret Garden

WHERE *Lavender Bay, Sydney* **WHEN** *In the winter, when the low sun shines beautifully through the plantings* **SIZE** *2.5 acres (1 hectare)*

Nestled over terraces and overlooking a pretty bay on the edge of Sydney Harbour, Wendy's Secret Garden was created as a path out of grief by a flamboyant and passionate gardener. The secret may be out, but this hidden garden remains a heart-warming gift to others.

Flowing among trees and over sandstone ledges, Wendy's Secret Garden lies hidden in plain sight below a sunny park and beside a busy road. Though this is a public garden, there's an intimacy here that makes it feel more like a private space. It is both.

A SENSE OF PURPOSE

Beyond Wendy Whiteley's home, railroad land had been abandoned for more than a century. In 1992, while struggling with grief following the death of her husband, artist Brett Whiteley AO, Wendy found herself in a dark place, and so threw herself into weeding, clearing, and planting this space. The land was public-owned, but she didn't ask permission, and no one told her to stop. Rather, she quietly worked on what she thought of as her secret garden, something that needed her care and attention to survive. When tragedy struck again nine years later with the death of her daughter, Arkie, Wendy turned to the garden with even more determination. The process was healing, almost meditative; it required her full attention and became a necessary distraction.

THE SECRET GROWS

Of course, Wendy's garden didn't stay secret for long. Passersby noticed what she was doing. Some stopped to help while others offered gifts of plants, and so the garden—and Wendy's spirit— grew. Wendy was no horticulturist, but she had imagination, filling the space with found objects, such as a sewing machine and an antique tricycle, and whimsical plantings. Mature Morten Bay figs and tall Bangalow palms tower above subtropical plants and native ferns. Paths lead to nooks, linked by small flights of stone steps with rustic handrails made from cut saplings.

The garden has iconic neighbors, and thousands of commuters thunder by each day on trains, but tucked out of sight, the garden remains a place of protection. Daily, Wendy and visitors come to take a breather on benches, meander aimlessly, and, ultimately, heal. Though Wendy has always worried that her garden would be threatened by development, the local council secured a 30-year renewable lease. Thankfully, her garden can continue to provide peace and solace to those who need it.

Right
Divine views of Sydney Harbour Bridge from the garden

Far right
Red Gymea lilies, native to eastern Australia, in front of Wendy's home

IF YOU LIKE THIS

Chelsea Physic Garden

UK • EUROPE

Hidden behind high
brick walls on the banks
of the Thames, this
"secret" healing garden
was established as a place
to grow medicinal plants.
Today, it contains a living
collection of around
5,000 plants that have
changed the world,
including some that are
vital to modern medicine.

ITALY · EUROPE

Giardini la Mortella

WHERE *Via Francesco Calise Operaio Foriano, Forio, Ischia* **WHEN** *Spring and fall, to catch the delightful chamber music season* **SIZE** *5 acres (2 hectares)*

Lady Susana Walton's jungle paradise was created as a quiet refuge for her husband, composer Sir William Walton. Yet what started as a testament of love for her husband became Susana's own passion project—a magical, tropical oasis born for, and created in, harmony.

La Mortella is a living monument to three creative minds of the 20th century: garden designer Russell Page, plantswoman Lady Susana Walton, and composer Sir William Walton. When the Waltons bought the property on the island of Ischia in 1956, the arid hillside was nothing more than a deserted quarry. Page, a friend of the couple, was brought in to design a garden, but it was Susana's passion for plants that turned it into a lush retreat. It was here that William composed some of his most famous music, shrouded in tranquility and nature at its finest.

A TALE OF TWO GARDENS

Divided into two parts, La Mortella's vegetative exuberance and botanical variety is rivaled by few gardens of southern Italy. Upon entering, visitors find themselves in the shady, humid intimacy of the Valley Garden. At its heart lies a large, egg-shaped lily pond, where an elegant water jet shoots up and mists the plants around it. It's then a climb up to the light-filled Hill Garden, a haven of native holm oaks, olive trees,

and a layer of cistus and fragrant myrtle, all growing in and around rock outcroppings. La Mortella is a garden to journey through nonchalantly, up and down stairways to nooks and crannies where peaceful moments await.

The older valley area is still home to many of the tropical and subtropical plants that Susana added to the property half a century ago. She was a hands-on supervisor of all the works that made the garden so extraordinary for its time and location. The tropical look serves as a reminder of her homeland Argentina but is botanically the result of a colorful, worldwide mix of lush vegetation and aquatic plants, including tree ferns native to Australia, African papyruses, and Nile lilies. A silk floss tree (which Susana grew from seed gathered in Buenos Aires) now shades the brightly colored bracts of bromeliads, begonias, and fuchsias. In the greenhouse, orchids bloom and giant leaves of *Victoria amazonica* float on the water's surface. Everywhere there is abundance, exuberance, and Susana's spirit—her *joie de vivre.* →

LABOR OF LOVE

Susana wasn't the only one with a passion for the garden. Page continued developing and expanding the design for years, never once submitting an invoice for his work. The addition of a fountain and water troughs to celebrate William's 80th birthday in 1983 was his last contribution to La Mortella; that same year, William died, and, two years later, Page, too. Despite the passing of her husband and dear friend, Susana persevered with the garden they had all loved so much. The Hill Garden was entirely her creation, and she accented it with a teahouse from Bangkok that sits among bamboo and hibiscus.

It is no coincidence that Susana had William's ashes enshrined within a pyramidal, solid stone boulder monument high in the garden. He rests in peace in a place that offered him just this: a favorite spot on their property, from where sweeping views look down over the sun-drenched Mediterranean landscape. After her death in 2010, Susana's ashes were interred where she stipulated they should remain—in her beloved nympheaum, surrounded by the garden that she cherished with all her heart.

MUSIC PLAYS ON

Today, in peak visiting seasons, there's certainly less of an intimacy and tranquility at La Mortella than when this was a private hideaway. Yet William's wish was never for La Mortella to remain a secret. His greatest dream was to help talented young musicians, and the garden has been doing this ever since his passing. Trusts in England and Italy provide funding for concerts and master classes held here, helping the garden serve as a theater for symposiums that celebrate musical, intellectual, and artistic creativity. When events are on, paved paths are bordered by not only thousands of plants but hundreds of people. Yet no matter what, relaxing moments are never far away—benches offer moments to take a breath, and intimate corners wait to be found while exploring.

———

FOCUS ON

Music Events

A Greek theater situated at the heart of the Hill Garden is a spectacular stage for symphonic concerts held on summer Thursdays, performed by the Festival of Youth Orchestras. Behind, stunning views of the island beyond make these concerts even more special.

———

The garden's intention remains the same as it did in 1956: to capture the beauty of art, nature, and music and act as a tribute to Page's passion, William's success, and Susana's talent as a plantswoman and gardener. Indeed, the classical music concerts and, at times, lively atmosphere keep the garden—and memories of William and Susana Walton—very much alive.

Clockwise from top left
Steps leading to peaceful nooks

Hillside gardens affording grand vistas over the island

Pink-purple clusters of blooming Geranium maderense

Huge Victoria amazonica *floating in the greenhouse*

Jardins de Métis

WHERE *200 Route 132, Grand-Métis, Quebec* **WHEN** *First two weeks of July when thousands of the blue poppies are in bloom* **SIZE** *45 acres (18 hectares)*

This surprising garden, cut out of a winding spruce forest, is the stunning result of one woman's doggedness and passion. Jardins de Métis—also known as the Reford Gardens—has become one of the most celebrated gardens in Canada, a place to lose yourself on meandering paths.

Philanthropist Elsie Reford never expected to become a gardener, but after an operation at 53, the outdoorswoman was told by her doctor there would be no more fishing, hunting, and equitation for her. Instead, he suggested she take up gardening. Initially reluctant, she gave it a go and ended up turning the estate around her remote salmon fishing lodge into a vast garden.

Reford learned through action. Her major difficulty, other than the frigid local climate, was a lack of arable soil. To overcome this, she traded salmon that her guests caught for peat, soil, and leaf mulch from nearby farms. Unable to do any heavy lifting, she brought in local men to spread the soil and move heavy rocks, trees, and shrubs. Lacking any local nursery, too, she had to grow nearly all her plants from seed ordered by mail, and rely on perseverance and experiment.

A QUIET SPLENDOR

This garden may have been a way for Reford to keep busy, but it's become a place to slow down and take stock in. This is a garden to be discovered step by step, passing from the Blue Poppy Glade with its startling hues, through the riot of reds, yellows, and oranges of the Azalea Walk before reaching the majestic Long Walk, with its wide beds of peonies, lilies, roses, phlox, and more.

FOCUS ON

Blue Poppies

Reford was one of the first people to grow the Himalayan blue poppy (*Meconopsis betonicifolia*) in North America, importing seeds shortly after its introduction in 1926. Today, the striking blue flower is the emblem of the garden.

Jardins de Métis remains, after nearly 100 years, a family affair. Today, the gardens are maintained by a foundation headed by Reford's great-grandson, Alexander, ensuring that the family name—one that brings to mind a renowned plantswoman—will long be remembered.

Above
*Reford's iconic
blue poppies
incorporated
into the Blue
Poppy Glade*

Left
*Meandering
paths leading
through
densely
planted
woodlands*

Spirited Garden

WHERE *75 Nokchabunjae-ro, Hangyeong-myeon, Jeju* **WHEN** *From March to May, when the weather is most pleasant and spring flowers are in bloom* **SIZE** *10 acres (4 hectares)*

A philosophy of love, understanding, and communion with nature inspired this gorgeous garden on the South Korean island of Jeju. The Spirited Garden is a display of what humans and nature can achieve together and, ultimately, a place to find peace of mind.

The word "gardener" does not do Seong Beom-yeong, the creator of this garden, justice. He is an artist of the arboretum, and his garden's beauty is that of the art of bonsai—tiny trees trained to mirror the intricacy of their species in microcosm. There are some 400 such trees across this garden; they line rivers studded with stepping stones, adorn quiet pergolas with purple wisteria, and render the air fragrant with the scent of lemon and tangerine.

A LABOR OF LOVE

Wandering this garden is not just to be in awe of Seong's talent but his determination. A Korean pig farmer, he would visit Jeju frequently, eventually buying barren land to build a garden on. Bonsai reflected his philosophy on life—that beauty can come from pain, and he hoped that his garden and its trees could contribute to world peace. Though a huge ambition, the garden certainly instills a sense of wonder in visitors, especially when surveying the love and care with which Seong rears his plants.

In the Juniper Garden, the quiet dignity of 300-year-old trees creates a poignant atmosphere for meditating on the conflicts between Korea, China, and Japan, outlined on information boards. Beside it, the Philosophy Garden is home to *dol hareubangs*—stone statues found throughout Jeju island that bestow blessings and protection, installed to encourage reflection on the COVID-19 pandemic. Everything is done with purpose and painstaking patience, inviting visitors to see that beauty and the peace it brings takes time but is endlessly worthwhile.

TRY IT AT HOME

Grow a Bonsai

Begin by buying some "nursery stock" of a tree that suits your local climate. The trick to keeping the tree miniature is pruning and wiring—wrapping metal around branches to dictate how they grow.

Clockwise from top
Carefully pruned bonsai trees dotting one of the eight garden areas

Water gushing down into a pond

Dol hareubang stone statue sitting along a pathway

If a garden is a place to celebrate the natural world, then nothing does that quite like the wild garden. Forget order and restraint; in these gardens, it's about honoring nature for what it is—untamed and exuberant. When left to do its thing, nature is truly incredible, whether it's letting wisteria cascade over derelict ruins or witnessing beguiling cacti pepper the desert with rich hues of yellow, pink, and purple.

AN EXPERIMENTAL SPIRIT

Paradoxically, of course, no matter how spontaneous they may seem, few gardens are ever truly wild. Naturalistic gardens that harness the natural aesthetic are very much curated to do so. If the wider landscape appears as though it is part of the garden, it's the result of arduously blending together wildflowers, grasses, and cultivated species. Ultimately, it's about experimenting—mixing formal and informal planting styles, knitting together layered plants, and, for the likes of garden designers Mien Ruys and Piet Oudolf, adhering to the naturalistic design style of the New Perennial Movement.

For some, experimentation is less about trying out new plant compositions and more a case of transferring their conceptually "wild" imaginations into their landscapes. Edward James, for example, let his artistry run wild when he carved a Surrealist jungle landscape from lush rainforest, where climbing plants tangle around and between architectural structures. Ganna Walska, meanwhile, paired the theatrical with the horticultural, stirring the imagination with odd statues and animal topiary in different corners of her characterful garden.

WILD AT HEART

The wild garden is not all about aesthetics, though. Experimenting can simply mean seeing what plants can bloom in seemingly uninhabitable climates. Think nothing can grow in the far north of Norway or North America's searing desert? The gardens created in these extreme temperatures prove that a lot can—dazzlingly colorful plants and all. Letting nature thrive on its own—or with little intervention—also goes a long way in protecting indigenous species. How lucky are we, to have gardens in the likes of South Africa and New Zealand where we can marvel at nature's rare bounties?

To some degree, what all wild gardens have in common is a boldness, be it in the planting style or the general concept. They are certainly all wonderful showcases for how astonishing nature can be on its own terms.

ŌTARI-WILTON'S BUSH

NEW ZEALAND

HERMANNSHOF

GERMANY

TUINEN MIEN RUYS

NETHERLANDS

LAS POZAS

MEXICO

BILTMORE GARDENS

US

GANNA WALSKA LOTUSLAND

US

KIRSTENBOSCH NATIONAL BOTANICAL GARDEN

SOUTH AFRICA

LE JARDIN PLUME

FRANCE

TROMSØ ARCTIC-ALPINE BOTANIC GARDEN

NORWAY

DESERT BOTANICAL GARDEN

US

LA THOMASIA

SWITZERLAND

GIARDINI DI NINFA

ITALY

THE HIGH LINE

US

Ōtari-Wilton's Bush

WHERE *150 Wilton Road, Wellington* **WHEN** *September and October to see the kowhai, rata, and Chatham Island forget-me-nots in flower* **SIZE** *12 acres (5 hectares) of botanic garden set within 247 acres (100 hectares) of indigenous forest*

Richly forested and beautifully curated in a natural setting, Ōtari-Wilton's Bush holds the largest collection of New Zealand native plants in the country. Internationally, it is one of the few gardens that concentrates solely on indigenous flora.

A passion for New Zealand's native flora is fundamental to everything that happens at Ōtari-Wilton's Bush. Originally, this garden was part of a swathe of forest that provided a hunting ground for the Māori Indigenous peoples, but by 1840, European settlers arrived and set about clearing the tall rainforest. Local farmer Job Wilton, however, was so appalled by the wholesale clearance of the land that he fenced off 17 acres (7 hectares) of it, determined that some of the "bush" would escape the axe. This tract of unfelled forest was to form the basis of a more extensive reserve established in 1926 by Dr. Leonard Cockayne, New Zealand's greatest botanist.

AN ODE TO NEW ZEALAND
Cockayne was so anxious that the country's indigenous flora be preserved that he set out to develop a purely native collection. At the botanic garden, sumptuous plants from the subtropical north happily coexist with rare species from the sub-Antarctic islands. Sitting beyond and below this are ancient and regenerating forests, where epiphytes perch in branches and supplejack vines dangle across valleys. A walkway across the deep forested gully provides intimate peeks into the canopy of tall trees, interspersed with sweeping vistas of bush-covered hills. It leads to the rock garden, the undisputed gem of the collections with its rich mix of herbaceous and shrub species.

Almost every plant in this reserve has been raised from cuttings or seeds collected in far-flung corners of New Zealand. Once established, many of the plants are propagated by Ōtari's green-fingered gardeners and then planted back into the wild. This is conservation in action.

1,200
The number of species of native plants, hybrids, and cultivars growing at Ōtari-Wilton's Bush. This includes the locally extinct maukoro (*Carmichaelia williamsii*).

Clockwise from top left

*Carmine rata
(Metrosideros carminea)
adding color to
the landscape*

*The tough, narrow, barbed
leaves of the juvenile
lancewood (Pseudopanax
crassifolius)*

*Overlooking native bush
that has never been felled
from the viewing platform*

GERMANY · EUROPE

Hermannshof

WHERE *Babostrasse 5, Weinheim, Baden-Württemberg* **WHEN** *Late April for spring tulips
and wisteria, September and October to see the grasses at their peak* **SIZE** *5.7 acres (2.3 hectares)*

Whether you're new to naturalistic-style gardens or an ardent follower of the New Perennial
movement, Hermannshof will open your eyes to the wild beauty of habitat-based planting,
practiced here at its highest level with aesthetics, ecology, and low maintenance in mind.

When you come to Hermannshof, bring a camera, a notebook, and an added dollop of your capacity for wonder. Here, in one all-encompassing botanical garden, you can roam freely between an amazing array of naturalistic garden borders, each modeled on one of the diverse natural habitats from temperate regions around the world.

LEARNING FROM NATURE

Hermannshof was originally the private estate of the Freudenberg family, wealthy industrialists who purchased the land in 1888. By the late 1970s, the future of this grand estate and its gardens had grown uncertain. As a solution, friend of the family and notable landscape architect Gerda Gollwitzer suggested turning Hermannshof into a demonstration and trials garden. Such gardens typically test how various plants perform in plots row after row.

Instead, Hermannshof set out to show how to effectively associate plants according to their respective habitat to create a more informal naturalistic style of garden.

The project took wing, based on seminal research by Professor Richard Hansen, who studied the habitats of perennials in the wild to develop an ecological approach to planting them successfully in gardens. This was a radical idea in an era when flowers were planted on the basis of aesthetics. Hansen then passed the baton to his protégé, Professor Urs Waller, who drew up the first planting plans for the garden and became Hermannshof's first director.

GARDEN HABITATS

Waller applied Hansen's ecological principles to create a series of distinct garden habitats within Hermannshof, with the plant list for each matched to its specific conditions. →

The end result was not only scientifically rigorous but a thing of great beauty. In the south side of the garden, a sinuous wood chip path leads into the junglelike environs of a lush East Asian woodland, festooned with ferns and shade-loving herbaceous perennials. An open expanse of dry prairie showcases flowers and grasses from the North American grasslands and Eurasian steppe, blended seamlessly into one mesmerizing and dynamic whole.

Hermannshof is best known for its masterfully designed plantings of perennials, grasses, and geophytes that create intrigue and atmosphere year round. Spring explodes in an abundance of color here, with thousands of tulips, narcissi and *Camassia* all timed to bloom on cue with emerging stands of *Malus*, *Cercis*, and magnolia. In summer, the borders are at their fullest with steppe and prairie plantings blooming in turn. In the annual border, edible *Amaranthus*, cosmos, and zinnias provide a rainbow of color. Though the palette is more muted, prairie grasses and seed heads dazzle well into the fall and even winter months in a wash of burnished copper and golden hues.

CULTIVATING THE NEW GERMAN STYLE

Hermannshof opened to the public in 1983, setting a new benchmark for garden knowledge in Germany. Visit the garden today, and you will see the profound creative influence of the garden's current director, Cassian Schmidt.

Over the past 20 years, Schmidt has designed an evocative new series of wild landscapes inspired by his global travels as a plant hunter. On a practical level, he has put greater focus on maintenance, or rather, the lack of it. His ecological planting system obtains maximum results in minimal time and with minimal effort.

FOCUS ON

Plant Communities

Plants are social creatures. Professor Hansen introduced the idea of plant sociability from his observations of species in their wild habitats. Some plants prefer to be solitary, while others thrive in small groups or large colonies.

You can see the full effect of this approach in his majestic prairie fields, which may look wild but are, in fact, cleverly planted in a deep layer of quartzite gravel to minimize the need for constant weeding.

This New German Style seeks to be both functional and beautiful, and Hermannshof certainly delivers on both fronts. This truly spectacular garden shows us that taking inspiration from natural habitats can inform planting decisions for the better.

Clockwise from top left

Masses of tulips bringing a bold splash of color in the spring

Purple wisteria growing along the pergola walk

Echinacea lighting up the dry prairie planting

Plant hunter and garden director Professor Cassian Schmidt

**Clockwise
from top left**
*Intermingled
perennials
and grasses
in the Sun
Borders*

*Ferns and
water lilies
gracing
the canal
by the barn*

*The Ready-
to-Wear
Borders
offering ideas
to implement
at home*

Tuinen Mien Ruys

WHERE *Moerheimstraat 84, Dedemsvaart, Overijssel* **WHEN** *Spring through fall to witness beautiful blooms* **SIZE** *6.2 acres (2.5 hectares)*

Not just one, but 30 highly imaginative garden spaces make up Tuinen Mien Ruys. Arranged in chronological sequence, they chart the experimental nature and life work of Dutch landscape architect Mien Ruys, who introduced a distinctly wild aesthetic to modern garden design.

Visiting Tuinen Mien Ruys is like walking through a timeline of ideas, for this is where Mien Ruys—often cited as a major inspiration for the New Perennial garden movement—worked for 70 years, exploring radical new ways to build gardens. Ruys always had a deep knowledge of plants, having grown up next door to her father's Moerheim Nursery. Yet it was studying garden architecture briefly in her early adult years that got her thinking about the materials used in gardens, which were as key to her as the plants themselves. Combining her two passions, she began to create small gardens on her father's land, experimenting with new combinations of plantings and materials.

EXPERIMENTAL BY NATURE

A creative aesthetic is visible across all 30 garden rooms. In her first experiment, The Wilderness (1924), Ruys accentuates shade-loving perennials with simple geometric paths. In this marriage of rigid hardscape and loose plantings, a straight path of stone tiles leads to a square pond, shaded by trees and surrounded by naturalistic woodland planting. It's a practical landscape, too: the layered perennials suppress weed growth while the leaf foliage enriches the soil with humus to create what Ruys called a "controlled wilderness."

Ruys was adept at layering perennials—chosen for their differing shapes and texture—to give them a wilder character. Throughout the gardens, they're intermingled in small groups, creating natural-looking drifts that appear spontaneous—an effect that is contrasted with the defined frame of an architectural structure like exposed aggregate tiles, decking, or railroad sleepers. In the Standard Perennial Border (1960), the plantings, counterpoised by minimalist hedges, transform the garden into a canvas of ephemeral wild beauty. Ruys's work may have inspired a whole movement, but it's the functionality of her landscapes that inspires those who visit, prompting us all to get creative with our own gardens—no matter how small.

TRY IT AT HOME

Wild by Design

Follow Ruys's example and do away with your lawn in favor of a designed layout with stones, specimen trees, and minimalist hedges. Experiment with industrial materials in your hardscape, too, like steel and cinder blocks.

---

*The jungle
encroaching on
the Bamboo
Palace, one of
the Surrealist
structures*

MEXICO · CENTRAL AND SOUTH AMERICA

Las Pozas

W H E R E *Xilitla, San Luis Potosí* **W H E N** *March–May, when the flowers begin to bloom
and before the summer heat sets in* **S I Z E** *80 acres (32 hectares)*

In the remote, jungle-clad hills of central Mexico, Las Pozas is a Surrealist fantasy of a garden
dotted with beguiling—and sometimes baffling—works of art. This subtropical wonderland,
which the jungle seems determined to reclaim, is the result of imagination run wild.

As you follow the rough-hewn paths that meander through the labyrinthine, subtropical sculpture garden of Las Pozas, a succession of bizarre structures emerge from dense foliage. Have you stumbled upon a lost city, abandoned by some ancient civilization centuries ago? Not quite. Look closer—a flight of stairs leads only to the sky, a collection of rooms stand without walls, an erratic scattering of giant-size rings, archways, and colonnades litter the ground. This is more larger-than-life Surrealist art installation than forgotten ruin— and that's precisely what the creator of the garden intended.

Las Pozas was the brainchild of Edward James, a British poet and artist whose eccentricity was matched only by his wealth. Born in 1907 into a family that made a fortune from railroads and copper mines (though rumored to be the illegitimate son of King Edward VII), James had a traditional upper-class upbringing but was quick to take his own path as an enthusiastic patron of the Surrealist art movement, which was then in its infancy. He spent time in the United States and later traveled to Mexico. Determined to find a bucolic spot where he could focus on his writing, he was eventually drawn to the small, picturesque town of Xilitla on the mist-shrouded slopes of the Sierra Gorda. Captivated by the area's rugged beauty and sweeping views, James bought a large, jungle-covered plot of land just outside of the town in 1944. He wanted a Garden of Eden, and over the next four decades, he let his imagination run away as he created his idiosyncratic wonderland.

AN ORCHID OBSESSION
With the help of his friend Plutarco Gastélum Esquer, James built his home on the site and set about creating his paradise. For a while, he was focused on horticulture, introducing into his garden thousands of varieties of orchid from around the world. In 1962, however, a snowstorm struck, all but destroying James's treasured collection. →

"Typically one has to clear
vegetation in order to build.
Here the opposite was true.
[James's] architectural intervention
in nature served to highlight
its fertility and variety."

IRENE HERNER, ART CRITIC

James was devastated by the loss of his beloved orchids and decided to create something that couldn't be killed in their place. Inspired by his passion for the revolutionary artistic movement, he set about fashioning what was to become his very own Surrealist wonderland.

THE THREE-STORY HOUSE THAT MIGHT HAVE FIVE

Taking advantage of Xilitla's plentiful supply of inexpensive labor and Mexico's loose building regulations, James spent the next 20 years designing more than 200 artworks, sculptures, follies, and buildings for his Surrealist garden, despite lacking any architectural or engineering experience. Built from concrete and reinforced steel, these structures initially took the form of flowers (including imitations of the orchids he had lost), plants, fungi, leaves, and trees, before becoming increasingly fantastical in appearance.

Many of these follies still stand today. As you wander through Las Pozas—with the sound of birdsong, flowing water, and the gentle hum of insects emanating from the greenery—you will encounter towers, columns, arches, bridges, elevated walkways, and spiral staircases, often stacked perilously on top of one another and left open to the elements.

One such structure, tangled with vines, is the vertiginous multiterraced Three-Story House That Might Have Five, which stretches up to the forest canopy. The cobbled Road of the Seven Deadly Sins, meanwhile, features representations of humankind's darkest peccadilloes and is guarded by a menacing mosaic of snakes. Form trumps function every time in this "Surrealist Xanadu"—a term James used to described his garden—and many of the structures echo imagery found in works by Salvador Dalí and other Surrealist artists.

1,000

The amount in US dollars that James spent every week on building materials and employing a team of laborers, workers, and craftsmen for his projects at Las Pozas.

AN ENCROACHING JUNGLE

That's not to say this garden is all about its sculptures. No, the surrounding jungle is an essential and active presence in Las Pozas, despite James's efforts to keep the invading foliage at bay. The plantings appear untamed and, in places, even wild. There are myriad varieties of trees here, some native, others introduced by James himself. Vying for attention are *Delonix regia*, more commonly known as "flamboyants" and boasting a shock of bright orangey-red flowers; *Pseudobombax ellipticum*, nicknamed the "shaving brush tree" on account of the appearance, when freshly opened, of its wispy white flowers; and *Cordia elaeagnoides*, stately Mexican rosewoods. →

Clockwise from left

*The cobbled Road of
the Seven Deadly Sins*

*Gates opening to
reveal cascading
waterfalls and plants*

*Thick foliage
engulfing James's
Surrealist structures*

Alongside these are coffee plants, banana and mango trees, bromeliads, and several large species of fern, which range in color from pea green to a deep burgundy. Natural elements of the landscape—most notably a cascading river that has created a series of idyllic waterfalls and pools (from which Las Pozas takes its name, literally translated as "the pools")—also play a central role in the garden's design.

DOORS TO NOWHERE

James's playful sense of humor and wild imagination shines through at Las Pozas, which has plenty of visual jokes: the cinema lacks seats and a screen, the library has no books, and many of the doors cannot be opened—and those that do lead to nowhere. These sit alongside mosaics of snakes, a sculpture of a pair of giant hands, and frescoes of minotaurs by the British-Mexican Surrealist artist Leonora Carrington, whose work James championed.

Over the years, mosses and lichens have spread across the surface of the structures, giving them the appearance of centuries-old ruins, while fast-growing foliage laps around their bases like an incoming tide. It is hard to know where the forest ends and Las Pozas begins, so seamlessly have they meshed together. Few of the buildings were ever finished and only one—James's own residence—was habitable. As the guides here explain, the garden was always a work in progress, with James constantly tinkering, redesigning, and adding new elements.

A SURREALIST DREAM

Las Pozas fell into neglect and a state of disrepair following James's death in 1984, with the jungle becoming ever more entangled with the buildings and sculptures. Thirteen years later, Las Pozas was purchased for $2.2 million by the Fondo Xilitla, who bought the site to conserve the sculptures and to protect the surrounding land and gardens. The foundation carried out extensive restoration work and opened it to the public in 1991.

Today, a guided tour of Las Pozas is both a magical and a faintly melancholic experience, a reminder of the power of imagination and the lack of time to realize your dreams. It makes you appreciate James's ambitious plans and singular vision of the world. He was "crazier than all the Surrealists put together," Dalí reportedly said. "They pretend, but he is the real thing."

IF YOU LIKE THIS

Inhotim

BRAZIL ·
CENTRAL AND
SOUTH AMERICA

This botanical garden
and open-air art gallery
near Belo Horizonte
showcases works by some
of the world's leading
contemporary artists
such as Yayoi Kusama
and Matthew Barney.

Biltmore Gardens

WHERE *One Lodge Street, Asheville, North Carolina* **WHEN** *Spring, when the flowers and trees are in bloom with bold and brilliant colors; and fall, when the colorful change of leaves across the mountains creates an awe-inspiring view* **SIZE** *30 acres (12 hectares) of formal gardens, part of the 8,000-acre (3,237-hectare) estate*

Shaped by two American visionaries, this is a real transformation of land from agricultural use to pastoral landscape. At Biltmore, formal and informal gardens blend together, with lawns, meadows, and forest sweeping across the horizon.

Looking at Biltmore today, with its rolling meadows and manicured gardens, it's hard to imagine how it looked when George W. Vanderbilt II purchased land here. Vanderbilt, a member of one of the wealthiest families in the US, was familiar with the area of Asheville, visiting it frequently with his mother. He loved the fresh air and impeccable views so much that he decided to buy a staggering 125,000 acres (50,585 hectares) of land—including farms—on which to build an estate.

A NOVEL DESIGN

Though vast, the land Vanderbilt acquired had its faults: the mountains had been denuded of trees by lumber companies; pasture land had become overworked; and the soil was so poor, little would grow in it. In 1888, he contacted the preeminent landscape architect of the day, Frederick Law Olmsted, to create a plan for the land. At first, Vanderbilt envisioned building a public park around his home, but Olmsted noted that the topography was unsuitable for this vision. Instead, Olmsted convinced him to take on a bold new idea: rebuild the forest and return the land to a more natural setting. To do so, his plan was to create sweeping views to the river and the mountains to be admired from the house, farm the land adjoining the river to keep livestock and make the rest a forest.

Vanderbilt was enthused by the idea of preserving the forest still standing, while also making it productive to acquire timber. →

FOCUS ON

Frederick Law Olmsted

Known as the father of American landscape architecture, Olmsted (1822–1903) created many of America's top public gardens and parks. His first project was designing New York City's Central Park, and Biltmore was his last.

The rolling hills of the French Broad River Valley surrounding the sculpted Walled Garden

1888

George W. Vanderbilt II begins purchasing land near Asheville, North Carolina, to build a grand estate and home.

1888

Frederick Law Olmsted travels 24 hours by train from New York to Asheville to start work on the design of the gardens and forest landscape.

1889

Vanderbilt begins construction of the Biltmore house, completed six years later.

1914

Vanderbilt dies; his wife, Edith, sells 87,000 acres (35,200 hectares) of land to the US government to create the Pisgah National Forest—the first national forest east of the Mississippi River.

1963

Biltmore becomes a National Historic Landmark.

Impeccable views from the house across the rolling meadows and dense forest to the mountains

On Olmsted's recommendation, he hired forester Gifford Pinchot to develop a plan. A cycle of harvesting and replanting was adopted to create a healthy forest for future generations—the first such forest management plan in the US.

Meanwhile, Olmsted focused on the design. While the palatial home was being built, he created a 3-mile (5 km) long Approach Road from the estate's entrance to the house, which he deemed integral to one's experience of the garden. Today, the road winds through a forest that looks as if it were made by nature but was actually created by Olmsted out of bare land. Plants were positioned as nature would have placed them—smaller ones closer to the road and larger shrubs and trees in layers behind

these set in an irregular pattern. Olmsted believed that natural scenery had a powerful effect on people needing to unwind and also built miles of walking, hiking, and biking trails that also looked natural but were, of course, perfectly planned.

THE GARDEN FROM THE TREES

The beauty of this sprawling garden is the way in which the wilder forest area blends seamlessly with the more formally manicured gardens in front of the house. Once Olmsted had finished the road leading up to the home, he began turning the 30 acres (12 hectares) surrounding the house into gardens. The resulting landscape—gardens connected by paths that wind through

the trees—is a dreamy world of time stood still. The centerpiece of the formal gardens is the Walled Garden, where 50,000 tulips woven together like a carpet bloom in April and May. To the north, the Azalea Garden—the largest of Biltmore's gardens—is filled with native azaleas collected by the estate's first superintendent, botanist Chauncey Beadle, who would spend

130,000

The approximate number of flowers that grace the estate's gardens during *Biltmore Blooms*—an annual flower festival that takes place every May.

weekends driving through the southeastern US searching for every species, natural hybrid, and color of azalea. Here, some 20,000 plants spill out along paths, creating a brilliant display with over one million blossoms in springtime colors.

A WALK TO REMEMBER

Not knowing where the commissioned garden ends and the natural landscape begins is the crux of Biltmore's spectacular appeal. As a new generation hikes the forest-covered mountains and strolls between the rolling meadows and curated gardens near the house, they are enveloped into the world of the majestic Blue Ridge Mountain setting that spoke to Vanderbilt more than 100 years ago.

Left *Azaleas brightening Biltmore in hues of red, pink, and orange*

Right *Tall plants dominating the glass-roofed Conservatory*

Ganna Walska Lotusland

WHERE *695 Ashley Road, Santa Barbara, California* **WHEN** *July and August, when the lotuses are in bloom in the Water Garden* **SIZE** *37 acres (15 hectares)*

Tropical plants, whimsical garden settings, and merry eccentricity combine to form fantastical Lotusland, a magical creation by former Polish opera singer Madame Ganna Walska. Over 3,000 noteworthy plants represent the extraordinary horticultural passion of one remarkable woman.

Filled to the brim with exceptional plant collections, Lotusland is a sensory delight. Creating such a unique botanical nirvana requires a wonderful imagination, and that's exactly what Walska had when she bought the sprawling estate in 1941. "I am an enemy of the average," she once declared, and her creative planting style certainly attests to this.

DRAMATIC DESIGN

Over four decades, Walska created a flamboyant land, blending the traditional with the theatrical. She grouped species en masse and placed serene water features and amusing sculptures among willfully wild plantings. Walska was not a hostage to practicality. Rather, she experimented with bold plants and unusual color combinations.

More than 20 different garden themes dot the landscape. One of Walska's first projects, the plantings in front of her pink stucco house, features towering masses of gold barrel cactus and the stately *Euphorbia ingens* succulent. In contrast, the Topiary Garden, affectionately referred to by Walska as her horticultural zoo, features neatly clipped animals, from a giraffe to a peacock. By further contrast, the Water Garden comes alive in the summer with the garden's namesake lotuses—a sight for sore eyes.

In her taste for the unexpected, Walska ensured her garden offered something surprising and new at each turn. In one corner, she planted a Japanese garden; in another, an Australian garden; elsewhere, an Italian-style parterre with Spanish and Moorish elements. This is certainly a garden that has as much character as the woman who created it.

450

The number of species in the Cycad Garden, the last garden created by Walska, who financed the rare plants by auctioning off her jewelry.

Clockwise from top
Looking out across the lotus-filled Water Garden

Water cascading from a giant clam shell fountain into the Abalone Pond, the Aloe Garden

An immense collection of towering cacti in the Cactus Garden

Kirstenbosch National Botanical Garden

WHERE *Rhodes Drive, Newlands, Cape Town* **WHEN** *May to November, when the proteas, leucadendrons, pincushion proteas, and serrias are in bloom* **SIZE** *1,304 acres (528 hectares), with 89 acres (36 hectares) in cultivated gardens and the remainder in natural forest*

The wild beauty and diversity of rare flora found in Kirstenbosch is unlike any other place on earth. Created on the eastern slope of Table Mountain in Cape Town, Kirstenbosch preserves, propagates, and displays a remarkable range of plant species indigenous only to South Africa.

The inviting Camphor Avenue, lined with the evergreen Cinnamomum camphora

When neglected farmland in Cape Town was donated to the South African government in the early 1900s, local botanists were at the fore, urging for the creation of a garden where the preservation of native vegetation could take place. After all, botanists had discovered that Cape Town was the most biodiverse city in the world, home to 20 percent of Africa's flora, including 200 species not found anywhere else. Building Kirstenbosch provided a rare opportunity to showcase this flora.

Plans to create the garden were implemented in 1913, and the vast scrubland began a transformation back to its more natural *fynbos* (fine bush) landscape. The area was cleared of the nonnative trees and shrubs that had overtaken the land, and an infrastructure of paths, bridges, and buildings was added to the landscape. Some of the early plants grown here were of economic value—cork oaks, olives, castor oil—planted for both research and to raise money, since government funds were not enough to keep Kirstenbosch going. Botanical society members and the public were even asked to donate plants. As more money became available, other garden sections were added, including buildings and mass plantings of ericas, proteas, and showy annuals. →

FOCUS ON

King Protea

The king protea (*Protea cynaroides*) is the national flower of South Africa, native to the country. The largest of all proteas, it is often used to make a statement in floral arrangements. The Protea Garden in Kirstenbosch has many displays of king protea, which flowers mostly from June to October.

Lower sections planted with indigenous flora blend into a vast natural cover of native *fynbos* vegetation and forest at high altitudes. These natural areas make up 90 percent of the land, compared to just 7 percent for cultivated areas. Some 7,000 species indigenous to South Africa find a home here—restio, ericas, and wild gardenias—as well as threatened species like *Ocotea bullata* and *Widdringtonia wallichii*. Near the main entrance, a glass-topped conservatory houses plants that can't be grown outside: stone plants that look like the rocky surrounds, unusual cone-bearing plants found only in the Namib Desert, and the glorious centerpiece, a large baobab tree that is typical of the arid Kalahari. At the far end of the garden, native plants seemingly tumble down from the mountain, delightfully dense and thick with foliage.

A GARDEN OF GARDENS

Today, over a century after its creation, visitors certainly delight in Kirstenbosch's wonders. In the sprawling landscape, seemingly endless garden areas are linked by a network of foot-paths to be enjoyed by walkers and mountaineers. The aptly named Fynbos Walk, for instance, passes through colorful vegetation unique to the Cape—most notably, proteas.

This is a garden to be explored aimlessly, chancing upon hidden bounties. There's a Fragrance Garden, where aromatic flowers perfume the air; a Garden of Extinction, where some of the nearly 1,500 South African plants at risk live; and the Dell, the oldest section, replete with tree ferns and other shade-loving plants.

Perhaps the most thrilling area, however, lies to the west, where over 450 southern African tree species find a home in the Arboretum. Many of these, like Cape saffrons and a grove of tall forest myrtle quince, are from the subtropical regions of eastern South Africa and thrive on the warm north-facing slopes of Kirstenbosch. Winding its way above the Arboretum is the Centenary Tree Canopy Walkway, also known as the "Boomslang" (tree snake). Strolling between the curved steel railings, which look like a snake's skeleton, feels like venturing into the forest on the back of a snake. Such a novelty aside, this is also where you'll witness some of the most magnificent views of the wilds of Table Mountain meeting the cultivated gardens below. →

FOCUS ON

Cloud Spotting

Known as a "tablecloth over Table Mountain," the iconic mountain is often covered by clouds that quickly roll in off the ocean and spread across the flat top of Table Mountain. The clouds can also disappear as quickly as they appeared.

Top *Admiring the view above the trees from the Tree Canopy Walkway*

Bottom *Wandering along one of the many meandering paths*

TIMELINE OF EVENTS

1795

First time the name Kirstenbosch appears in property records, though not linked to any particular property owner.

1811

Kirstenbosch is divided into two halves and sold during the second British Occupation of the area. Colonel Christopher Bird, a deputy colonial secretary, buys the southern half and builds a bird-shaped pool known as Colonel Bird's Bath.

1895

Cecil John Rhodes purchases Kirstenbosch. He dies in 1902 and his will gives the land to the South African government.

1913

The government sets aside Kirstenbosch for a National Botanic Garden on the urging of botanists.

1927

A record 2,841 plants are added to Kirstenbosch.

2014

The Centenary Tree Canopy Walkway opens.

**Clockwise
from top**

*Aloe thriving
against the
backdrop
of Table
Mountain*

*The
flourishing
Cycad
Amphitheatre*

*Lance-leaf
sugarbush*
(Protea
lanceolata)

Higher up, Table Mountain itself provides an ever more epic view of the land. It's possible to hike up the mountain from within Kirstenbosch on the Smuts Track up Skeleton Gorge, which starts near the Fragrance Garden and follows Skeleton Stream, and includes a steep ascent that should be hiked with caution. If the weather allows, scramble up rocks, climb ladders, and take in the breathtaking scenery on a five-hour loop to witness nature at its finest.

HISTORIC HORTICULTURE

For all its beauties, Kirstenbosch is a garden entrenched in history. Many of the oldest and most historic sections are linked on the Heritage Trail, a 1-mile (2 km) self-guided route marked with directional signs and storyboards. One of the most notable stops on the route is Van Riebeeck's Hedge, a jumble of intertwined native wild almond trees (*Brabejum stellatifolium*) and roots that resembles an enchanted forest. Planted here in 1660 by Jan van Riebeeck, the commander of the Dutch East India Company, these trees marked the controversial boundary of the new Cape Colony.

Indeed, reconciling with the past is an ongoing part of this garden. Recognizing its connection to the Indigenous peoples and plants that lived on the land long before settlers arrived is key to Kirstenbosch's

21st-century mission. As such, in 2003, the Useful Plants Garden opened with the consultation of traditional healers and Rastafari *bossiesdokters* (bush doctors). It features 150 labeled plants commonly used in indigenous southern Africa for practical purposes, including cereal plants and vegetables, as well as plants for crafts, weaving, and dyes, and for medicinal uses like easing stomach aches and colds. Today, Kirstenbosch works to be a place of all South Africans, weaving in the stories of those whose voices were lost along the way.

FOCUS ON

Sculpture Garden

Sculptures in the garden showcase the many faces of Africa. The rotating exhibit of Mambo sculptures made by Zimbabwe artists in the Shona tradition reflect spiritual, traditional, contemporary, and social issues that have dominated the continent for centuries. Meanwhile, animal bronzes by South African artist Dylan Lewis are a nod to the wild nature of the country.

Top *Informal plantings surrounding the old barns*

Bottom *Rounded topiary contrasting with playful perennials*

Next page *Tall, airy perennials and grasses set against the iconic wave hedges*

Le Jardin Plume

WHERE *790 Rue de la Plaine, Auzouville-sur-Ry, Normandy* WHEN *Late June for the Feathers of Summer plant festival; mid-September for Les Plantes de L'Automne* SIZE *7 acres (2.8 hectares)*

Designed as a love letter to classical French garden design with a highly contemporary twist, Le Jardin Plume will seduce you with its wild feathery plantings set loose within a playful structure of dragonback hedges, impeccable topiary, and minimalist orchard oases.

On the flat windswept plains just outside Rouen, keep a sharp eye out for the hand-painted arrow that directs you off the road and into the self-contained garden universe of Le Jardin Plume. From the moment you arrive, you are enveloped in the Gallic charm of the half-timbered French farmhouse and its imaginative planting styles. A tension between formal and informal elements is at the root of everything designed and planted here.

A GARDEN OF IDEAS

Le Jardin Plume is the creation of husband and wife Patrick and Sylvie Quibel, who set out to create a garden inspired by André Le Nôtre (*p12*), the illustrious landscape architect of Louis XIV, and American naturalistic design masters Wolfgang Oehme and James van Sweden. Their garden and its myriad areas is a synthesis of contrasts and extremes, with Baroque principles transposed into wild yet modern dreamscapes.

In the Orchard Garden—the centerpiece— the couple transformed the farmhouse's former orchard and sheep pasture into a *grande allée* of apple trees. Its wide mowed paths lead down an expansive grid of diamond-cut squares sequenced with an early flush of spring bulbs and wildflowers. Alongside these, unmowed lawns are left to grow wild. There are two reflecting pools for skyward contemplation, surrounded by tall grasses that come fully into their own by the fall. To the right, in the Feather Garden, the rising crests of the wavy boxwood hedge frames the flowers and feathery grasses that give Le Jardin Plume its name. From a distance, it would be easy to mistake the nearby Summer Garden for a traditional box parterre. Yet closer up, dazzling blooms in yellow, red, and orange burst from the confines of every neatly trimmed box hedge. Order and disorder blend together beautifully at every turn.

Le Jardin Plume is themed by season, each area a jewel box of wildly intermingled plantings set within geometrically sculpted hedges—a veritable mélange of design. This juxtaposition shouldn't work. But it all makes perfect sense in a garden where control and unrestraint purposefully live in harmony.

Tromsø Arctic-Alpine Botanic Garden

WHERE *Stakkevollvegen 200, Tromsø* **WHEN** *April to see the very first flowers breaking snow cover, or June to stroll through an eruption of blooms under midnight sun* **SIZE** *4 acres (1.6 hectares)*

The world's northernmost botanic garden, Tromsø Arctic-Alpine Botanic Garden honors the untamed and unexpected, cultivating a global collection of vibrant, graceful blooms in a rigid rock face. Only within its cool, craggy crevices can its unusual collection thrive.

If ever there was proof that gardens can thrive in the most extreme of climates, it is this botanical garden, perched between shining fjords and snowcapped peaks in the far north of Norway. Despite lying inside the Arctic Circle, Tromsø does not have a fully arctic climate, allowing this garden to bloom. It enjoys bright summer nights with midnight sun and the perpetual darkness of the winter, but the seasons are milder due to the mitigating effects of the Gulf Stream, giving Tromsø a longer growing season than expected, from May to October.

BARRENNESS AND BEAUTY

Tromsø Arctic-Alpine Botanic Garden was once farmland belonging to teacher Hansine Hansen. Before passing, she bequeathed her property to the public for education, and in 1994, Tromsø University opened an insular garden on the site dotted with arctic plants. Free from fences, the garden is divided into regional and botanical collections by boulder walls, gravel paths, and stony assemblages, evoking the sparse terrain where its more than 2,000 plants originate.

A highlight of the brightly colored landscape is the tallest rock flower bed, embedded on a ridge in the garden's southern perimeter. With maximizing habitats in mind, botanists planted the warmer ridge side with species like yellow Patagonian cushion plants. The Arctic collection, meanwhile, dominates the ridge's cooler side. Here resides Europe's endangered Svalbard buttercup (*Ranunculus wilanderi*), whose clusters of tightly packed buds seem to spring from cold stone. This buttercup is a diminutive emblem of the garden's inspiring overarching theme—no matter how sparse the terrain nor how challenging the climate, there's a bloom that can thrive in this land.

700

The number of plants in the large North Norwegian Traditional Garden, all brought in from old gardens of the region. It includes dusky magenta saxifrage (*Saxifraga cotyledon*), Norway's national plant.

Clockwise from top
The flinty landscape serving as a rough canvas for alpine plants

Mountain and boreal flora sprouting from rocks

Brightly colored varieties dazzling in garden beds

Desert Botanical Garden

WHERE *1201 North Galvin Parkway, Phoenix, Arizona* **WHEN** *Spring is best, when the cacti and wildflowers are in glorious bloom; midsummer can be brutally hot* **SIZE** *140 acres (56 hectares)*

Trails snake through a surreal world in this cactus-filled sanctuary, nestled in the Sonoran Desert. Accented with fuzzy chollas, snakelike ocotillo, and Arizona's signature saguaros, this inspirational raw, untamed, xerophytic oasis defies the image of the desolate desert.

When Swedish botanist Gustaf Starck posted a sign to "save the desert" outside his home in the 1930s, a group of visionary cactus lovers teamed up to do just that. It was Starck and local socialite Gertrude Webster who led the way in creating a botanical garden, a way to save a prime swatch of desert from urban encroachment. Their legacy is a globe-spanning showcase of more than 50,000 xerophytes—plants adapted to survive long periods of extreme heat and drought without ill effect.

WONDERS AWAIT

Taking any of the garden's five thematic loop trails, it's easy to gain a newfound respect for the desert. This is not a place of tumbleweeds but rather one that brims with the glories of nature. Flaunting Sonoran cacti and succulents in three ascending landscaped terrace-gardens, the beguiling Ottosen Entry Garden sets the stage for the wilder garden experience beyond. Accessed by a grid of pathways, each garden here is an evocative vignette with a distinctive combination of stone and desert plants: prickly pears, organ pipes, barrel, and red cholla cacti.

Moving further into the garden, the 0.25-mile (0.4 km) Sonoran Desert Nature Loop Trail thrills the most, circling through an archetypal wild local landscape. Here, the cactus family has reached a pinnacle of diversification. Stands of organ pipe cactus and hulking—and rare— saguaro probe skyward. Peer closely at the ground and you may spot a pincushion cactus, barely 2 inches (5 cm) tall.

COLORFUL HUES

As well as its diverse plant life, the garden surprises with its beautiful palette. Following winter rains, it bursts into riotous color, with wildflowers blossoming in spring. Bees gather pollen amid the yellow-blooming paloverde, and hummingbirds flit about the cactus flowers. →

186

The number of the world's 212 known agave species displayed in the garden, making this the largest such collection in the US, if not the world.

Clockwise from right
Yuccas blossoming with clusters of bell-shaped flowers

Mountains looming behind the garden

Prickly pears bursting into bloom

IF YOU LIKE THIS

Karoo Desert National Botanical Garden

SOUTH AFRICA · AFRICA

A grand collection of South African succulents, especially vygies (ice plants), blossom en masse in spring.

The Huntington Desert Garden

US · NORTH AMERICA

One of the world's oldest and largest assemblages of desert plants is the pride of this Pasadena botanical garden.

Purple lupines, pink Parry's penstemon, orange California poppies, and red tubular chuparosa blanket the desert floor. The Desert Wildflower Loop Trail unfurls 0.3 miles (0.5 km) through a section quilted with ground-hugging wildflower species, plus Sonoran flowering cacti, trees, and shrubs. Subsections here highlight the beauty and diversity of the flowering flora of the Chihuahuan, Mojave and Great Basin deserts.

DESERT AT NIGHT

As the air cools and night draws in, the garden takes on yet another character. Bats, moths, and other nocturnal critters emerge from their hiding places, and, in season, night-blooming cardon, cereus, organ pipe, and saguaro flowers exquisitely perfume the air. The Desert Botanical Garden stays open into the evening, tempting visitors to linger for the molten sunset and evanescent enchantment of the desert at dusk. Then, the garden is illuminated and the cacti and succulents take on a spectral presence. At no time is this seen better than during Las Noches de las Luminarias—a holiday tradition on certain nights in November and December when trails are lined with luminaria bags, twinkling like stars in the night sky. In summer, visitors shine a light on night-blooming plants and animals during Flashlight Nights, illuminating the wonderful flora and fauna that define the Desert Botanical Garden as a wild and parched, yet bountiful, landscape teeming with life.

1939

A small group of local citizens dedicated to desert conservation create the garden to protect a large swathe of natural environment from Phoenix's rapid urban spread.

1950s

The garden's collection expands from a mere 1,000 specimens to more than 18,000 under the directorship of cactus expert W. Taylor Marshall.

1979

The Las Noches de las Luminarias event is introduced, when 8,000 candles inside faux paper bags flicker alongside the trails and roaming mariachis entertain.

2008

The Ottosen Entry Garden opens as the first phase of a $17 million, 20-year redesign

2017

A new and expanded Butterfly Pavilion opens with more than 2,000 live butterflies native to Southwest US.

Tall saguaros standing behind barrel cacti, chollas, and Yucca rostrata in the Desert Terrace Garden

La Thomasia

WHERE *Pont-de-Nant, above Les Plans-sur-Bex, Vaud* WHEN *Between June and August to see the flowers in bloom* SIZE *3 acres (1.2 hectares)*

Untamed nature and Swiss precision exist in harmony at La Thomasia. Situated in a mountain pasture overlooked by toothy peaks, this high-altitude garden offers a snapshot of alpine flora from around the world. Journey from Japan to Canada to Nepal, all without leaving Switzerland.

On visiting La Thomasia, overlooked by the Grand Muveran mountain and bordering the wild Nant valley, it isn't hard to imagine why people were once afraid of the Alps' unchartered wilderness. By the 19th century, however, fear turned to pride: the Alps were mapped and developed, and in 1891, the Bex town authorities decided to create an alpine garden to show off the beauty of the mountains.

A LIVING MUSEUM

Ernst Wilczek, a local botanist, was tasked with developing the garden. His creation is a microcosm of the world's alpine flora, planted across a series of rockeries that each reflect a different mountainous region. A stream winds around and between them, its calming trickle overlaid by the furious rush of the nearby Avançon de Nant river. Around the perimeter, organic growth encroaches on selected plants, making it hard to see where human intention ends and nature takes over.

With a little under half of the garden's surface area left wild and occupied by a spruce forest, there is no wish to dominate or tame the natural environment, only to work in harmony with it. It's an approach spearheaded by Wilczek, who wanted his garden to be more than just a tourist attraction. He gave it a scientific dimension by planting threatened species such as Edelweiss and tested the ability of certain food sources to grow at altitude. Today, La Thomasia continues to learn from the environment it inhabits, indicating why we should not fear the alpine wilderness but respect and preserve it.

4,133

The altitude in feet (1,260 m) of La Thomasia, which benefits from a unique microclimate due to the presence of surrounding mountains like the Grand Muveran.

Nestled at the foot of the Grand Muveran, the garden offers lovely views over the Nant valley

"Plants are historical documents of our country's natural history and deserve to be preserved as much as old buildings do."

ERNST WILCZEK

ITALY · EUROPE

Giardini di Ninfa

WHERE *Via Ninfina 68, Cisterna di Latina, Lazio* **WHEN** *For an abundance of rambling roses, tumbling wisteria, irises, and wildflowers, April and early May are as good as it gets; the garden is only open to the public on selected days from March to November* **SIZE** *20 acres (8 hectares)*

The lush plantings that cascade over the crumbling ruins of the medieval town of Ninfa have earned this place a spot among Italy's most romantic gardens—a bold claim but one that it is indeed difficult to dispute.

Rambling roses, fragrant racemes of wisteria, meadows brimming with wildflowers, and a crystal-clear river that flows through the land—here all are contained within one ruined medieval town. Weeds fill cracks in crumbling, sun-baked walls where lizards scamper in search of shade. There is nowhere that combines the magic of ancient buildings with the exuberance of nature quite like Ninfa. From its stone ruins to sparkling rivulets of water, all is kept in check to give the impression of a gloriously wild space where nature reigns over all else.

RICHES TO RUIN

In the early 14th century, Ninfa was an important town, with a castle, churches, towers, a town hall, and nearly 2,000 inhabitants. By the end of the same century, it was well on its way to becoming a ruin, surrounded by swamps and pillaged by mercenaries, having been sacked and razed to the ground in 1381. What Pope Boniface had bestowed upon the noble Caetani family in 1297 soon became an overgrown ghost town, forgotten by most. It would be another 600 years before Ninfa would be awoken from its deep slumber. →

264

The speed in gallons per second at which Ninfa's river flows, creating a microclimate for temperate plants that would otherwise not survive Italy's Mediterranean summers.

Clockwise from top
*The hilltop town of
Norma overlooking
the garden*

*The spring-fed river
bordered by irises, calla
lilies, acanthus, and roses*

*Roses adding a splash
of color to Ninfa*

A FAMILY LEGACY

When creating a naturalistic garden in an ancient site, it is often difficult to balance the somewhat conflicting desires to rebuild and renew with a sentimental longing to allow the moldering ruin, or in this case entire town, to rest and show its age. How much should be left to gracefully deteriorate? It was ultimately up to the Caetani to decide.

In the early 20th century, Prince Gelasio Caetani and his mother, English noblewoman Ada Bootle-Wilbraham, began the clearing and restoration of Ninfa's ancient bridges and crumbling buildings, including what would be the main residence on the property, the former town hall. They solidified some of what was sure to fall and created canals and a stream out of the stagnant waters.

These were just the first steps to transforming Ninfa. Their work was followed by that of Gelasio's brother Roffredo and sister-in-law Marguerite. Between them, their tasks were divided: Roffredo worked on designing, creating, and maintaining the bones of the garden, while Marguerite added her favorite plants. Roffredo and Marguerite's son, Camillo, who was heir to the estate, died in World War II, but his sister, Leila, and her English husband, Hubert Howard, took over the property and brought it closer to the dreamy English landscape garden that we see today.

WILD, FLORIFEROUS NINFA

Despite such intervention, Ninfa's luxuriant combination of flowering trees, shrubs, and perennials create a spontaneous effect that feels somehow natural and unplanned. The fake ruins and follies that became fashionable on the grounds of regal estates in the 18th century have no place here. The ruins here are very much real, massive, and scattered everywhere; history pours from their weathered stone, and the garden has consumed them, repurposing bridges and walls for its own use.

———

FOCUS ON

Lauro Marchetti

The current curator for the Caetani Trust, Lauro Marchetti is the man behind much of Ninfa's magic. Now in his 70s, he has worked on the property since he was a young boy, when he was a protégé of Hubert Howard and Leila Caetani. He knows the trees and plants of Ninfa like the back of his hand, every creature and feature.

———

Of course, no garden is truly spontaneous. The soft, romantic English garden atmosphere of Ninfa does not look or feel artificial because it has been so consummately created. But one thing is for certain: its century-old trees and ancient hoary walls continue to provide the most exquisite supports that thickets of climbers and vines have ever had the joy of clambering up and cascading over.

The High Line

WHERE *Meatpacking District, West Chelsea, New York City, New York* **WHEN** *Fall, when the golden prairie grasses and seedheads are at their most captivating* **SIZE** *926 acres (375 hectares)*

Once an abandoned railroad viaduct destined for demolition, the High Line is now an elevated public park and rail trail that leads visitors through a visionary postindustrial landscape of naturalistic gardens, soaring architecture, and audacious art.

A wide stairway, flanked by massive riveted girders and beams, marks the High Line's southernmost entrance on Gansevoort Street in New York City's now fashionable Meatpacking District. Not just any stairs, these are slow stairs, designed with a shorter rise and longer tread to slow your pace as you ascend to the botanical wonderland that awaits.

By the time you reach the glass railing at the top, you are on the High Line proper, three stories above the city in the welcoming shade of the Gansevoort Woodland. From here, a planked concrete pathway leads through a tranquil thicket of white multistem birches poking up vertically from between the wooden ties of rusted steel rail tracks that are dotted with sedges and ferns. In spring, this honey-scented woodland dazzles with the flowering of early blooming shrubs like *Cornus*, *Amelanchier*, and *Cercis*. If you are fortunate enough to visit in fall, the collective foliage turns all shades of golden yellow, deep vermillion, and burnished copper—a spectral supernova that you certainly don't want to miss.

Of course, this is no ordinary woodland. A glance up through the trees reveals the cantilevered steel outlooks of The Whitney Museum of American Art. And as you emerge into the Washington Grasslands and Woodland Edge, sight lines open up to embrace a spectacular 360°-degree panorama with the skyline of Manhattan in the near distance and the Hudson River off to the west. →

FOCUS ON

The High Line Effect

The revamp of the High Line attracted a wave of architectural innovation, with buildings by some of the world's foremost architects now situated on either side of the park. Marvel at the work of Frank Gehry, Zaha Hadid, Renzo Piano, and Todd Schliemann, among others.

Clockwise from top
Strolling along the elevated pathway

A river of green flowing through the city

Echinaceas and feather grasses rising up between the concrete runners

"The gardens of the High Line are designed to create a feeling of wildness and romance. At the same time, they invite people into a different way to garden and teach them to see gardens from another perspective. Seasonality and process are the keys here."

PIET OUDOLF, LANDSCAPE AND PLANTING DESIGNER

Next page *Prairie wildflowers in the grasslands glowing in the early evening sun*

A NEW YORK STORY

The High Line was built in 1934 as an elevated freight railroad line to service the West Side of Manhattan, replacing a street-level train line with a dismal safety record. The trains on the High Line transported goods like dairy, meat, and produce to factories and warehouses along the tracks of its north–south route. The railroad was operational for nearly 50 years until the rise of the trucking industry forced its demise.

The immense concrete and steel structure stood abandoned for two decades, during which time nature took hold. Weed seeds blew in from across the river, turning the railroad line into a clandestine oasis of wildflowers and urban habitat. New York photographer Joel Sternfeld captured the strange beauty of this derelict world in an iconic photo essay for *The New Yorker* in 2000, directing everyone's attention to it.

Pressure built from local residents to tear down the eyesore but two members of the community saw it differently. In 1999, Joshua David and Robert Hammond formed the nonprofit group Friends of the High Line in an attempt to save the structure. After they won the support of incoming mayor at the time, Michael Bloomberg, the group launched an international design competition in 2004 with the goal of repurposing the High Line into a public park for all to enjoy.

SIMPLE, WILD, QUIET, AND SLOW

The winning entry did not seek to change the High Line. Quite the opposite, in fact. The design intent was to preserve the spirit and integrity of the structure, inspired by its found conditions. This was to be a collaboration between James Cormer Field Operations, architectural firm Diller Scofidio + Renfro and Dutch planting designer Piet Oudolf. Their aim was to create a slow park, greenway and rail trail to honor the site. In doing so they developed a design language inspired by the industrial form and function of railroads, which influences the design of the entire hardscape from the peel-up benches, intended to resemble raised sleepers, to the restored steel guardrails.

The design involved removing all the existing materials, including the railroad tracks. These were later replaced in their original position. To build the promenade, they installed concrete planking along the length of the structure. The plantings run right through the tracks, tapering out to evoke the wildness of the original space.

After three years, the first section of the High Line opened to the public in 2009, and it continues to evolve in phases, ever expanding in exciting new ways. Designed to unfold like a story, every step brings with it new perspectives. The effect is an experience that feels like wild nature in one of the most hyper-urban places on earth. And that is what the High Line is all about—an elevated encounter with the essence of nature in a city of more than 8.5 million souls.

9,000,000

The average number of people who visit the High Line every year, making it the most popular tourist destination in New York City.

URBAN OASES

It might be a houseplant or a window box, a nearby courtyard, or patch of woodland; there's always a piece of green out there that you can happily call your own. And isn't that the best thing about gardens—the simple pleasures they offer us? Nothing evokes joy quite like witnessing a cactus grow ever so slowly on a windowsill, nurturing a tomato plant in your community garden, or listening to birdsong every lunchtime in the garden at the end of your road.

WORKING WITH LIMITATIONS

Even in the world's smallest places or most overdeveloped of cities, plants and flowers have a place. A garden needn't be on a plot of land rooted into the earth—it can spring from the most unlikely spaces. Where one person sees a derelict old water reservoir, a garden designer sees a canvas for an inner-city green space where weary shoppers can soak up the sun. An unused rooftop? Reclaim it and fill it with vegetation and water streams that block out the sounds of the bustling streets below. A glass-fronted office building? Create a vertical garden that's both visually beautiful and full of benches that invite

people to catch up among evergreens. And what about a vast airport? Add a dramatic rain vortex to its center and surround it with trees and nature trails, of course. Urban planners and landscape architects have shown us that dense city centers, filled with concrete and steel, are thoroughly amenable to the creation of natural environments.

A NEED FOR GREEN

Nature has the power to bring communities together, too. One of Berlin's favorite gardens—a community space where green-fingered locals grow vegetables and harvest herbs—is perhaps the city's least curated and pretty. Yet the pleasure it brings to a city where many people live in tiny apartments is tenfold. The same rings true in Colombia, where a botanical garden in Medellín becomes a communal living room for picnickers (as well as the likes of turtles and iguanas).

Better still, beyond what is easy to see, gardens boost a city's biodiversity, cool the air, and even trap particulate pollution. Really, is there anything gardens can't do for us—providing great pleasure, cleaning our air, and amazing us with their ability to thrive in the most unlikely of sites?

JARDIN MAJORELLE
MOROCCO

PALO ALTO GARDEN
SPAIN

LANDSCHAFTSPARK DUISBURG-NORD
GERMANY

JARDÍN BOTÁNICO DE MEDELLÍN
COLOMBIA

ST. DUNSTAN IN THE EAST
UK

PADDINGTON RESERVOIR GARDENS
AUSTRALIA

JEWEL CHANGI AIRPORT
SINGAPORE

PRINZESSINNENGÄRTEN
GERMANY

STEP GARDEN, ACROS FUKUOKA
JAPAN

UNIVERSITY OF WARSAW LIBRARY GARDEN
POLAND

Jardin Majorelle

WHERE *Rue Yves St. Laurent, Marrakech* WHEN *Year round, though the shoulder seasons of April to May and September to November are best if you want to avoid the intense heat.* SIZE *2.5 acres (1 hectare)*

Color is everything in the Jardin Majorelle. Here in the heart of Marrakech's Ville Nouvelle, vibrant blooms contrast with deep-blue backdrops, promising a welcome retreat from the city's stifling heat and frenetic energy. Step inside and enter the ultimate desert oasis.

One of the world's most famous gardens, Jardin Majorelle is instantly recognizable for its vivid color palette. It is hardly surprising then to learn that this leafy oasis is the work of an accomplished artist. French painter Jacques Majorelle (1886–1962) came to Marrakech in 1917 and, finding himself inspired by the city, purchased a plot on which to build his lasting legacy: a modernist studio surrounded by a luxuriant garden that now bears his name.

PAINTING WITH PLANTS

Majorelle's passion project, this garden united his two greatest loves: painting and planting. Neither Islamic nor French, it is a blend of styles from around the world, with trickling pools, fountains, and waterways that irrigate the land and soothe the senses. The shaded bamboo forest evokes an eerie beauty, while miniature landscapes lead the way to a lily pool bordered by flowering masses of bougainvillea, a scene

reminiscent of a Monet. Across the water, spiny specimens take on humorous shapes in the arid cactus garden. But it is Majorelle's daring use of cobalt blue—now known as Majorelle Blue—that has captured gardeners' hearts. Both warm and cool, this electrifying shade is the perfect backdrop for the towering cacti, palms, and profusions of tropical flowers that surround it.

MAJORELLE'S VISION LIVES ON

One of many to be enamored by the garden was French couturier Yves Saint-Laurent (1936–2008), who, along with his partner Pierre Bergé, rescued it after it fell into a state of disrepair when Majorelle died. In the skillfully restored garden that we see today, color is still present in every crevice: on the bright sunshine-yellow pots, in the deep blue of the studio, and along the meandering paths, dyed red to match the beaten clay buildings and ramparts of the "Red City" in which this urban oasis thrives.

Clockwise from right
*Striking blue
Art-Deco studio of
Jacques Majorelle*

*Orange trees lining
a tiled walkway*

*Colorful details marking
the entrance to the garden*

IF YOU LIKE THIS

Le Jardin Secret

MOROCCO · AFRICA

Divided into an exotic garden and an Islamic garden, Le Jardin Secret is another hidden oasis in the heart of Marrakech.

Joaquín Sorolla's Garden

SPAIN · EUROPE

Inspired by the Arabic gardens surrounding the Alcázar and Alhambra (*p58*), Impressionist painter Joaquín Sorolla's Madrid garden echoes the color palette of his work.

Bursts of
hot pink
and purple
bougainvillea
punctuating
the creeper-
covered walls

Palo Alto Garden

WHERE *Carrer dels Pellaires 30–38, Barcelona* **WHEN** *The first weekend of every month, when the Palo Alto Market takes over the complex with craft stalls and food stands* **SIZE** *Garden area: 0.7 acres (0.3 hectares); vegetation area (horizontal and vertical): 1 acre (0.4 hectares)*

A restored 19th-century textile factory in Barcelona's fashionable Poblenou district has been given a new lease of life. Its courtyard garden, with a dazzling profusion of plants arranged with an artist's eye, is an exuberant green retreat that invites creativity.

Gazing today at the walls carpeted in green, it's hard to imagine this was once a filthy, abandoned factory. It took the artist Javier Mariscal to imagine a future for it, transforming it into a creative hub with design studios in the 1980s. As artists began to fill the space, Mariscal turned his attention to the shabby courtyard. He brought in Josep Ferriol, a landscape designer, to shape a garden that would inspire creativity. With nothing but the succinct instruction to create "something green, something alive," Ferriol crafted one of the most enchanting havens in the city.

NATURE RUNNING RIOT

The old factory is a canvas for palms, ferns, and ficus—a visual poem to green in every texture. This isn't a garden to explore bed by bed or border by border, but a whimsical jumble of meandering paths with hidden corners and leafy bowers to discover at leisure. Pergolas are overhung with vines, the air is redolent with orange blossom in spring, and gold koi swim lazily in a tiny pond. It feels a world away from the hustle and bustle outside the courtyard. Here, the silence invites contemplation, and the colors, shapes, and smells ignite the imagination.

Designed for optimal biodiversity, the garden is home to more than 200 plant species. As a result, the air is cooler and cleaner within the complex walls than outside. This is, ultimately, a glorious green corner for the city and its citizens.

FOCUS ON

Smart Sensors

Created in 2012 by the Palo Alto Foundation and Fab Lab Barcelona, Smart Citizen Kits monitor the likes of air quality, acoustic pollution, and other key criteria for sustainability, collecting data to help improve the environment.

Landschaftspark Duisburg-Nord

WHERE *Emscherstrasse 71, Duisburg (Meiderich)* **WHEN** *In the summer or at weekends throughout the year, when evening light shows create a spectacular sight*
SIZE *570 acres (230 hectares)*

This former steelworks plant is now a place of urban beauty, where city dwellers come to enjoy extensive parklands, meadows, and waterways, all in the shadow of Blast Furnace 5, a haunting colossus of the heavy industry that once dominated the Ruhr district of Germany.

Upon entering the factory gates of the landscape park, your eyes are drawn upward by the specter of Blast Furnace 5, rising 236 ft (72 m) above like an industrial cathedral. Its three concrete chimneys mark the core of the old Thyssen Steelworks and coal plant, which has been shuttered since 1985.

It took remarkable vision to transform this site into a destination green space. The aim of the project, headed by German architects Peter Latz + Partners, was to keep existing structures intact but to repurpose them in unexpected and imaginative ways. The result is a riveting masterclass in industrial style.

The blast furnace site is now something of an industrial wonderland, interspersed with vast gardens, water, and meadows. Visitors can explore the old iron furnaces, turbines, control rooms, and access viewing platforms. Concrete bunkers are now climbing walls. The old cinder railroad beds serve as a network of paths that lead to the cultural hub of the iron-plated Plaza Metallica. The former fuel holding tanks have become the Gasometer, the largest indoor scuba diving site in Europe, complete with a shipwreck.

Since opening in 2002, the Landschaftspark has completely upended the conventional idea that a park is somewhere pretty and green. It has inspired revitalization projects in Germany and around the world to recycle the ghosts of our industrial past and incorporate them into a spirited, more sustainable future.

FOCUS ON

Plant Detox

The design team turned to plants as a means to naturally detoxify contaminated soils and waterways. This process of phytoremediation utilizes green plants and their related microorganisms by filtering contaminants through their roots.

Top *Nature rewilding the industrial remains of the former steelworks plant*

Bottom *View from Blast Furnace 5's observation tower*

COLOMBIA · CENTRAL AND SOUTH AMERICA

Jardín Botánico de Medellín

WHERE *Calle 73 #51 D14, Medellín* **WHEN** *August, when the garden hosts spectacular orchid displays during Medellín's annual Fería de las Flores (Festival of the Flowers)* **SIZE** *32 acres (13 hectares)*

Colombia's vast biodiversity is exhibited in microcosm in the Botanical Garden of Medellín, where urbanites bask in the natural landscape with iguanas, butterflies, and thousands of orchids for company. Once in its folds, feel the city's pace slow down.

The land that this garden occupies has been Medellín's communal heart since 1913, when the Municipality of Medellín created the Forest of Independence here. This huge park not only preserved local botanical species but offered entertainment for locals who would row boats on the lake or play tennis in the courts. Five decades later, the park had fallen into decline, and it wasn't until 1968 that its fortune would turn around. Medellín was elected to host the World Conference on Orchids—fitting, given that Colombia is home to some 4,270 known orchid species, more than any other country. It made sense to revive the desolate park into a new green space that would shine a light on the city's botanical diversity and give locals a recreational space back. And so, in 1972, the garden opened for both the conference and city dwellers.

A TROPICAL DELIGHT

This botanical garden adds a much-needed touch of greenery to Colombia's second-largest city. Comprising a natural escape, its vast collections are divided into myriad zones: a lake showcasing the natural ecosystems of wetlands; a desert area housing plants that thrive in aridity; a palm garden emphasizing the beauty of these slender species. The highlight, however, is the José Jerónimo Triana Orquideorama. →

100

The number of native palm species that thrive in the botanical garden, including the Quindio wax palm, the world's tallest palm at up to 200 ft (61 m).

Providing a stunning entrance into the garden, this huge beehive-shaped structure shelters shade-loving orchids, as well as bromeliads, carnivorous plants, and ferns that nestle at the base of 10 steel-framed spiral trunks. Resembling a soaring bouquet of flowers, together these "trees" explode outward in hexagonal petals. Walking below it generates a sense of strolling in a shady tropical forest, enhanced by a latticed ceiling of slatted hardwoods that cocoon the trunks. Sunlight and rainwater filter down through this ceiling, as if from a forest canopy, to feed the greenery. At night, when the treelike structures are lit from below, the effect is simply electrifying.

PLANTS APLENTY

The garden as a whole is certainly a love letter to Colombia's vast biodiversity. Southward, the Orquideorama merges into the Bosque

---

Cardboard Palm

The garden protects 24 species of *zamia*—a critically endangered genus of fernlike antediluvian cycads. Most species are found in humid, tropical habitats but are highly adaptable. *Zamia furfuracea*, or "cardboard palm," is robust, quick growing, and sun-, heat-, and cold-tolerant, and is easily grown indoors or in a garden.

Tropical, which replicates a montane tropical forest—one of a dozen distinct rainforest types in Colombia, and well suited to Medellín's 5,000 ft (1,500 m) elevation. Bathed in greenish sunlight, a boardwalk trail wends through the multilayered space and its profusion of plant life. On the ground, understory vegetation is adorned with bromeliads and tree ferns; above, the forest canopy with its treetops fuse like giant umbrellas, transporting visitors far from the Andean city center. The air is cool and dank and alive with the musical whistles and screeches of birds. Gazing upward is to feel like a mere speck, in complete awe.

Beyond the tropical forest, a grassy, hillocky area holds the palmetum. With 289 palm species, about one-tenth of the global count, Colombia is considered *numero uno* in total species. The palmetum exhibits some 120, including the iconic and endangered Quindío wax palm (*Ceroxylon quindiuense*)—the world's tallest, and the national tree of Colombia.

CREATURES BIG AND SMALL

The garden's sheer beauty and impressive plant collections are humbling, but this is, ultimately, a garden for the city's inhabitants. Just like the Forest of Independence that came before it, the Botanical Garden of Medellín is intended to be a place for locals to come to slow down and rejoice in the natural land. Picnics are hosted on the grass, turtles sunbathe on the rocks, and the ubiquitous butterflies float overhead, adding more color to the already kaleidoscopic garden.

IF YOU LIKE THIS

Singapore Botanic Garden

SINGAPORE • ASIA

This tropical-themed garden is home to the National Orchid Garden, which displays over 1,000 species and 2,000 hybrids.

Myriad Botanical Gardens

US • NORTH AMERICA

The top draw at this Oklahoma park is the tubular Crystal Bridge Conservatory, with its towering tropical plants.

Missouri Botanical Garden

US • NORTH AMERICA

At the center of America's oldest botanical garden is the Climatron, a stunning greenhouse that supports dense tropical flora.

Top *Water lilies floating in the lake*

Left *Medellín's famous metro train shuttling past the gardens and city*

UK · EUROPE

St. Dunstan in the East

WHERE *St. Dunstan's Hill, London* WHEN *September–November, to enjoy the atmosphere on quiet, misty mornings* SIZE *0.2 acres (0.1 hectares)*

An ancient church reclaimed by nature, St. Dunstan in the East offers pure refuge. Lush trees and shrubs emerge from the ruins, creating a delightful hideaway in the City of London, where time stands still and the city's signature bustle melts away.

Perched on a hill just a few minutes' walk from the Tower of London, this garden keeps its beauties hidden until the moment you step inside its bounds. There, the sound of the traffic retreats, giving way to birdsong and leaves rustling. To be here is to be enchanted. Creepers clamber up the high, stone walls of the ruined church, occasionally reaching their tendrils around the tracery of the arched windows. From certain spots, you can see the Shard, the glassy tower that scrapes the sky, but the garden feels as if it belongs to another world; here, the past feels closer than the present.

GROWING FROM THE RUINS

Altered and extended since the 12th century, the church itself was one of the city's most prosperous—until, that is, the bombing of World War II. Although the tower and steeple survived, the authorities decided not to rebuild, and the church went out of ecclesiastical use. However, in 1967, a decision was made about what to do with the ruins: the City of London was to breathe new life into them by creating a garden. A few years later, plants were flourishing beneath the watchful gaze of the gothic church.

TRANQUIL SHADE

Even on the hottest day, the garden feels calm and restful. Oaks and palm trees provide shade, and white hibiscus flowers burst forth in late summer. Office workers lunch on wooden benches, and a fountain bubbles quietly in the church's former nave. Filled with evergreens, the garden has a timeless quality—a reminder that visitors have found solace here for centuries.

TIMELINE OF EVENTS

1100

The church of St. Dunstan in the East is first recorded (the name distinguishing it from St. Dunstan in the West on Fleet Street), making it one of the earliest Norman churches in London.

1666

The Great Fire of London sweeps through the city, destroying 87 out of 109 churches. St. Dunstan in the East survives, although the tower and steeple are damaged.

1701

Sir Christopher Wren builds a new tower and steeple. Unusually for Wren, he designs them in Gothic style, to match the medieval building.

1941

The church is badly damaged by bombs in World War II, although Wren's structures survive. The church authorities decide not to rebuild.

1971

The ruins of the church are turned into a garden by the City of London and opened to the public.

Nooks and crannies, cloaked in greenery, offering ample hideaways for weary Londoners

Paddington Reservoir Gardens

WHERE *251-5 Oxford Street, Paddington, Sydney, New South Wales* WHEN *The late afternoon to enjoy the light play on the structures at sunset* SIZE *0.2 acres (0.1 hectares)*

Beside and below one of Sydney's major thoroughfares, a garden of paradise has sprung from the bones of an old abandoned water reservoir. Seamlessly transformed from water supply to peaceful haven, the space is still a support for the city in its new role.

Below ground, the Paddington Reservoir lay uncared for and unknown for decades until the dawn of the 21st century, when the city of Sydney commissioned architects to convert it into a park. Where the council saw crumbling ruins, the architects were captivated by the site's potential: dramatic structures around which innovative plantings could thrive and where the public could find respite. The final garden, spread over two levels above and below ground, certainly retains the reservoir's heritage through a blending of old engineering and bold design.

SAVING HISTORY

The reservoir had been built with two separate chambers, reinforced with timber pillars, brick arches, and vaulting. To create the sunken park, the crumbling roof was removed, exposing what remained of the internal structure. The result is a romantic lost world draped with plants, with air, light, and greenery clinging to every surface.

A limited palette of modern materials was used in the transformation. Curved aluminum vaulting over the entrance steps echo the old brickwork below, raised viewing platforms overlook the sunken space from above, and concrete pavers form paths through the garden, inviting visitors to meander thoughtfully.

Indeed, there's plenty to marvel at. A square reflective pool, surrounded by Australian native trees, is a calming presence. Elsewhere, hanging trails of hibbertia drip from the walls and massed flax lilies create a sea of green. Patches of lawn provide space to relax in the sun and take in the ingenuity of those early engineers and the foresight of modern landscape design.

Right *Deckchairs inviting tired shoppers and workers to soak up the sun and take a breath*

Below *Open to the sky, the cathedral-like sunken garden with its soaring columns*

TIMELINE OF EVENTS

1866
Paddington Reservoir opens to supply water.

1899
Site is decommissioned and used for storage.

1990
Roof collapse sees site abandoned.

2006
Tonkin Zulaikha Greer Architects (TZG) and James Mather Delaney Design (JMD) create an urban green space.

2009
Paddington Reservoir Gardens opens.

Jewel Changi Airport

WHERE *Airport Boulevard, Singapore* **WHEN** *The complex is lush year round; visit after nightfall to see the light-and-sound show projected onto the HSBC Rain Vortex*
SIZE *33.5 acres (13.5 hectares)*

If you ever needed proof that nature can thrive in the unlikeliest of places, this is it. On entering Singapore Changi Airport's five-story interior garden, complete with tumbling waterfall and nature trails enshrouded in mist, the stresses of air travel soon become a distant memory.

This may be the only airport on earth in which travelers hope their flight is delayed, just so that they have more time to explore Jewel Changi's nature-themed wonderland. Here, an impressive array of gardens and nature trails are contained within a glass-topped toroidal dome through which light floods the ground-level Shiseido Forest Valley floor, as lush as any in the outside world.

So enticing is this indoor garden that many travelers make a layover specifically to visit its many attractions: the Canopy Park, Petal Garden, Topiary Walk, and vertigo-inducing Sky Nets, which allow visitors to bounce around high above the treetops. Of course, the real highlight is the mesmerizing HSBC Rain Vortex that tumbles some 130 ft (40 m) from an oculus in the domed ceiling. Fed by recycled rainwater, this endless sheet of water flows effortlessly—and for the most part splash-free—into a giant

plunge pool five stories below. Dazzling by day, at night the water becomes a screen onto which a spectacular light-and-sound show is projected. But as well as being aesthetically pleasing, the HSBC Rain Vortex also serves an important function. The sheer volume of water and the speed with which it falls work to naturally cool the surrounding environment.

ALL PATHS LEAD HERE

While most airports are a confusing maze of tarmac and terminals, here visitors find themselves gently guided to the main garden area. It may be ringed by a busy shopping mall, with monorails coursing silently above, but the greenery prevails and all other distractions, as alluring as they may be, recede. In this transient space of departures, arrivals, last calls, and lost luggage, the sounds, smells, and sights of nature offer a blissful respite.

Left *Water gushing from the HSBC Rain Vortex, the world's tallest indoor waterfall*

Next page *The terraced gardens brimming with trees and plants*

IF YOU LIKE THIS

Ford Foundation

US · NORTH AMERICA

At the heart of this New York building is a 12-story enclosed atrium garden, regarded as the first such garden to be configured at the center of an office building.

Albert Einstein Education and Research Center

BRAZIL · CENTRAL AND SOUTH AMERICA

The classrooms and laboratories of this Sao Paolo institution are centered around a domed-topped series of terraced garden courtyards, each abloom with native Brazilian flora.

Prinzessinnengärten

WHERE *Hermannstrasse 99–105, Neukölln, Berlin* **WHEN** *April to October, when the café and restaurant opens and serves locally grown produce in the outdoor dining area* **SIZE** *18.5 acres (7.5 hectares)*

Dreamy, manicured landscapes full of topiary and flowers aren't the be-all and end-all of the garden sphere. This working garden revels in its unprettified state, serving as a community space for city dwellers, and an important addition to the urban gardening scene.

Before splitting into two locations, Berlin's most beloved urban gardening project started life as a guerrilla gardening site in Kreuzberg in 2009. This offshoot, also known as Prinzessinnengärten Jacobi, is located within Neuer St. Jacobi Friedhof, a cemetery dating back to 1867. Yet the mood inside this vast green space feels more peaceful than sombre. While the land belongs to the cemetery association, the leasing agreement allows the community to develop unused areas until 2035, welcoming visitors and volunteer gardeners.

REIMAGINING CITY SPACES

We think of gardens as rooted into the ground and immovable, but here, that concept is turned on its head. The mobile raised beds dotted throughout are a hallmark of urban community gardens, offering the ability to put roots down while simultaneously being able to safely relocate if leases change hands.

The use of recycled materials throughout the plots also embodies a circularity mindset essential for the city's sustainable future. Here,

Berliners have the chance to get their hands dirty and go from learning gardening basics to being able to grow their own food. A wooden cottage functions as Prinzessinnengärten's HQ, surrounded by seedlings for sale and handwritten signs detailing the activities taking place. Open-air discussions, environmental workshops, and sessions on everything from wild herb harvesting to climate action are just a fraction of what this garden offers the community.

A PLACE FOR ALL

Sharing the central gravel path are children cycling to one of the open communal areas and locals filling up watering cans at one of the taps along the way. Between them all, visitors freely roam and discover what's growing, from colorful blooms to Swiss chard to strawberries, depending on the season. Indeed, Prinzessinnengärten is an idyllic spot to refuel and engage in a little existential reflection. Its unique setup serves as a reminder of key gardening lessons: that life is cyclical, and nothing is permanent.

Clockwise from top
Raised beds surrounding a communal area, overlooked by apartment buildings in busy Neukölln

Herbs growing in compost-filled sandbags

Climbing tomato plants and trees blocking out the city beyond

Top *The garden, nicknamed Mt. ACROS, rising high over the park before it*

Bottom *The burnished copper shades of fall taking over the Step Garden*

IF YOU LIKE THIS

Hundert-wasserhaus

AUSTRIA · EUROPE

Trees and shrubs meld with the very structure of this Viennese apartment building, conceived by Austrian artist Friedensreich Hundertwasser.

Musée du Quai Branly - Jacques Chirac

FRANCE · EUROPE

A series of informal gardens, streams, and groves seamlessly integrate with the buildings of this Parisian museum. The highlight is a vertical garden, created by botanist Patrick Blanc.

Step Garden, ACROS Fukuoka

WHERE *111-Tenjin, Chūō Ward, Fukuoka City* **WHEN** *Summer to witness swallowtail butterflies flit around or winter for bright red berries and the crisp silhouettes of the trees* **SIZE** *1.3 acres (0.5 hectares)*

In the heart of Fukuoka City, a woodland paradise sprouts from a futuristic office building, creating harmony between the adjoining Tenjin Central Park and the human-made structure. Together, they all form an integrated public space for people to meet and relax in.

Like many buildings in a city's commercial heart, three sides of the 14-story ACROS Fukuoka are sleek and glass-fronted. The south-facing façade, however, is a welcome surprise, entirely covered in dense greenery—a vertical garden built to satisfy public demand for more green spaces in Fukuoka's high-rise district.

On the ziggurat-like stepped terraces, stairs zigzag up through the garden. Ascending visitors stroll past native evergreens and herbaceous perennials, pausing for breath on benches while the soothing sound of falling water and birdsong drowns out the noisy city below. At the top, an exhilarating view across to Fukuoka Bay awaits.

SUSTAINING THE CITY

The garden is not just an oasis for locals; it's a sustainable feat that does good for its plantings and the city itself, too. Residual rainwater is captured so that no extra watering is necessary; prunings are turned into mulch, returning nutrients to the plant beds; no fertilizers or pesticides are used. Moreover, the garden helps keep the building cool in the summer and warm in the winter. The moisture released by the plants lowers the air temperature during heat spells and, on muggy summer nights, a refreshingly cool wind blows down from the garden. The Step Garden truly points the way to the future of urban gardening.

37,000

The number of plants, representing 76 species, originally planted in the Step Garden. This has increased to more than 50,000 plants and around 120 different species.

University of Warsaw Library Garden

WHERE *Dobra 56/66, Warsaw* **WHEN** *April for an eruption of spring blooms; October to see fall's burnished hues color the city skyline* **SIZE** *6.2 acres (2.5 hectares)*

A long, gradual ascent transports students and visitors from Warsaw's busy city streets to this tranquil rooftop oasis atop the university library. Here, visitors find themselves immersed in nature while gazing upon the exhilarating cityscape of Warsaw.

According to the Roman philosopher Cicero, if you have a garden and a library, you have everything you need. The University of Warsaw Library, then, has it all. Refusing to be contained, vegetation tumbles over the library's steel- and glass-clad walls, enticing those who look up to venture further. An exterior double stairway beckons, connecting the lower section of the garden to the upper section, its gentle central slope lined with generous plantings of lush greenery and a row of solar panels.

NATURE, BY DESIGN

Responding to growing urbanization and a lack of greenery in the city, Polish landscape architect Irena Bajerska designed this garden as a space where the people of Warsaw could experience the benefits of nature without leaving the city. While this rooftop garden has many attractions, including a stream vaulted by arching bridges, it's the 49 plant varieties that make the biggest impression. Every species was chosen for its ability to thrive in the varied Warsaw seasons. The broadly rectangular space up here is divided into quadrants of color—gold, silver, crimson, and green—connected to one another by red-brick pathways that skirt a reflective pool and meander past a dome-shaped arbor dense with growth. Lookout points offer spectacular views over the ever-expanding city beyond.

VALUABLE LESSONS

It's fitting that a rooftop garden that teaches visitors about the benefits of connecting with nature in the urban space should be located on top of a library, a place where knowledge is gained. This pocket of urban greenery serves as a reassuring reminder that nature and city-living are not mutually exclusive. In fact, green spaces can be a key part of urban life. Nature can take root just about anywhere, after all.

Clockwise from right

External staircase leading to the arboreal dome and roof garden

Visitors exploring the roof garden

Covered walkways providing a source of shade and intrigue

IF YOU LIKE THIS

Matthaei-Nichols

US • NORTH AMERICA

Adjacent to the University of Michigan's main Ann Arbor campus, this vast expanse features native Midwest plantings and a student-driven campus farm.

Fordham University Rooftop Garden

US • NORTH AMERICA

Atop the main building of Fordham's Lincoln Center Campus in New York is a geometric roof garden set with sculpture, greenery and outdoor rooms.

INNOVATORS
AND
INFLUENCERS

How do we truly define a garden? As we've seen, it's not always neatly ordered beds and blooms in green spaces; a garden can also be a sparsely vegetated rock landscape, a working vegetable plot, or an ancient church reclaimed by ivy. Gardeners have been pushing the boundaries for centuries. Take Versailles, the trendsetter of the French formal style. Or the Garden of Cosmic Speculation, whose allegorical landscape delightfully boggles the mind of everyone who passes through. Even the Desert Botanical Garden is influential, for proving that tumbleweeds aren't the only life in the desert.

INSPIRING PEOPLE AND PLACES

Part of the joy in garden making, for many, is in bending the rules and shaping new ones. For socialite Bevis Bawa, this meant creating a fantastical landscape of playful sculptures and dense plantings; for changemaker Christopher Lloyd, it was redefining planting styles by mixing the formal with the informal; and for visionary Jennie Butchart, it was turning a limestone quarry into a floral masterpiece.

But innovators needn't always be doing something wildly out of the ordinary or attention-grabbingly bold. The study of plants has been important through the ages, whether it's in a small botanical garden in Italy or a global research center on the outskirts of London. Today, there's always a forward-thinking garden looking at how plants can respond to earth's dwindling resources or encourage sustainability.

True innovation certainly looks to the future and aims to solve a problem. That might be through preservation to conserve a country's ethnobotanical heritage or protect species that are nearly extinct. Sometimes, it's putting aside your own desire for aesthetics and working with, not against, the elements, choosing plants that will prosper in a garden's climate. Gardens that put nature first—be it through using renewable resources or conservation work—actively explore how we can work toward a better future. No type of garden is more influential.

GARDENS OF THE FUTURE

It's an understatement to say that gardens have rapidly changed over the centuries. Back in the formal days of the 17th century, the thought of plants thriving on a rooftop above a public library would have seemed absurd—but not, perhaps, as nonsensical as an underwater garden. So what does the future of gardening look like? If gardens have taught us anything, it's that, well, exactly anything is possible.

THE EDEN PROJECT
UK

LAMBLEY GARDENS AND NURSERY
AUSTRALIA

THE JOHN FAIREY GARDEN
US

FLOATING GARDENS OF XOCHIMILCO
MEXICO

THE BUTCHART GARDENS
CANADA

BRIEF GARDEN
SRI LANKA

TOKACHI MILLENNIUM FOREST
JAPAN

GARDENS BY THE BAY
SINGAPORE

GREAT DIXTER HOUSE AND GARDENS
UK

ROCK GARDEN OF CHANDIGARH
INDIA

NEMO'S GARDEN
ITALY

ENEA TREE MUSEUM
SWITZERLAND

KEW GARDENS
UK

PHA TAD KE BOTANICAL GARDEN
LAOS

UNIVERSITY OF PADUA BOTANICAL GARDEN
ITALY

LIJIANG HYLLA ALPINE GARDEN
CHINA

Eden's immense greenhouses, the garden's defining image, inspired by bubbles

The Eden Project

WHERE *Bodelva, near St. Austell, Cornwall* **WHEN** *May–early July to enjoy the biomes and the outdoor gardens before the summer crowds* **SIZE** *30 acres (12 hectares)*

Flowers bloom, bananas grow, and a waterfall plummets beneath gigantic domes—this is a garden of the future. A true triumph of innovation, the Eden Project celebrates the importance of plants to the planet and inspires everyone to reconnect with nature.

From the moment you set eyes on Eden's eight spaceship-like domes, you know you have arrived somewhere very special. While strolling beneath its palm trees, it's hard to believe that until 1995 this land was a working china clay pit—a vast hollow devoid of soil. Somehow, Tim Smit spotted its potential to breathe life into his vision: to awaken our awareness of the fragility of the earth, the importance of biodiversity, and the need for sustainable living to ensure a better future. Its size, scale, and symbolic value made it the ideal place in which to create a "shop window" for the planet, where the world's most important plants are showcased.

The process of transforming the site began a year later, with Tim and his team overcoming all manner of obstacles with great imagination. The nutrient-deficient pit was laced with composted greenery, creating a rich soil that could feed a variety of plant life. The absence of a natural water source inspired an underground

FOCUS ON
Tim Smit

Born in Holland in 1954, Tim Smit started his career in the music industry as a composer and producer. In 1987, he moved to Cornwall where, together with his friend, the builder John Nelson, he discovered and restored the Lost Gardens of Heligan. The Eden Project began as a dream, and in 2012 he was knighted for his work.

drainage system that would collect rainwater for irrigation. When the Eden Project opened to the public in 2001, the site was unrecognizable. The scarred land glinted with giant transparent domes, within which flourished trees and plants from the earth's major "biomes," or life zones. It was, indeed, a garden of Eden. →

FRUITS OF THE EARTH

Joined by the grass-roofed Link building, each four-domed biome is a world unto its own. The first, the Rainforest Biome, is a steamy paradise of tropical plants that grow in jungles. Built on the sunny, south-facing side of the pit, it is perfectly positioned to absorb thermal energy and, with temperatures inside reaching 95°F (35°C), is the place to be on a cold Cornish day. On the treetop walkway, the Weather Maker exhibit invites visitors to journey through clouds and shelter from tropical rain, to learn how rainforests cool the planet. This may be the biggest biome, but a piece of rainforest of the same magnitude is destroyed every 16 seconds—a telling reminder of the scale of the effort required to save it.

The Mediterranean Biome is no less inspiring, where the familiar mingles with the lesser-known. Oranges, cotton, and aloe grow, responsible for feeding, healing, and clothing us. Another section here devoted to the vegetation of Western Australia contains a grass tree (*Xanthorrhoea sp*): a species so resilient it thrives in the nutrient-poor soil of the outback and responds to wildfires by bursting into flower. Everywhere dazzles with sheer diversity, reminding us that plants are our life force.

OUTDOOR INSPIRATION

Surrounding the biomes are glorious and extensive outdoor gardens. Seasonal borders, displays of crops like tea bushes (*Camellia sinensis*), and plants from the world's temperate lands have made the sterile slopes of the former china clay pit burst with color. Among the 3,000 varieties growing outside are wildflowers such as poppies, cornflowers, and ox-eye daisies, which feed vital pollinators like bees and butterflies. Indeed, Robert Bradford's *Bombus the Giant Bee* sculpture, sitting amid these flower beds, is testament to the huge impact such small insects have on providing us with food.

SUSTAINABLE INITIATIVE

If anything is at the heart of the Eden Project's mission, it's sustainability. It leads by example, down to the smallest detail: leftovers from the kitchen are used to make compost to feed its plants and are even turned into electricity.

FOCUS ON

Building Biomes

The double-layered steel biomes were adapted to fit the clay pit's shape before being anchored to the ground. The transparent covering is very light and allows ultraviolet light to penetrate, so the plants inside can thrive.

Alternatives to palm oil make up an exhibit in the Rainforest Biome, and recycled rainwater is used to irrigate plants, feed a waterfall, and even flush on-site toilets. At every turn, Eden inspires visitors to reflect on their own lifestyles and the changes they can make to benefit the planet.

Like the earth, Eden is ever-evolving. Drilling has already begun on a geothermal plant at the site, which will use thermal energy from the underlying granite to heat and power Eden. Smit also has plans to create new Edens across the world, turning this innovative Cornish garden into a global movement for sustainable living.

Clockwise
from left
*Tim Shaw's
Rites of
Dionysus
sculpture, the
Mediterranean
Biome*

*A gardener
at work in
the outdoor
gardens*

*Citrus fruits
flourishing*

Lambley Gardens and Nursery

WHERE *395 Lesters Road, Ascot, Victoria* WHEN *Late July to early October to see spring bulbs, and February to April for late-season perennials* SIZE *5 acres (2 hectares)*

Gardening against the odds, but with the elements, the trailblazing creators of this sustainable garden worked with the harsh climate in southeastern Australia, creating dynamic planting schemes that can cope with big temperature fluctuations and drought conditions.

Of all the areas that make up Lambley, the Dry Garden always seems to take unsuspecting visitors aback. In this hedged enclosure, tall olive trees and triffid-like *Echium* tower over mounds of lavender and swathes of euphorbia. This accomplished scheme was not created just for dramatic impact. The planting is also drought-tolerant, requiring next to no water, even in the hot, dry summer climate.

WORKING WITH NATURE

Plantsman David Glenn was running a nursery near Melbourne when he met artist Criss Canning, and together they bought an old stone farmhouse in flat land north of Ballarat. David had previously grown moisture-loving, mountain-origin plants like rhododendrons, but such species were never going to survive the harsh conditions of his new garden, caused by an ongoing drought and highs of up to 117°F (47°C) in summer. The solution? Not to fight nature by constantly coddling unsuitable plants but to create a truly sustainable garden by switching to flora from Mediterranean climate zones and specimens from dry regions. After some trial and error, David and Criss settled on a range of beautiful but hardy plants, such as sedum, which can manage not only heat in summer but also the intense cold of winter. The plants were watered once upon planting, and apart from this, the Dry Garden—and the Mediterranean Garden, just across the drive—might be irrigated only two to three times a year, if necessary.

There are other areas that don't receive such tough love, however, and need watering in dry spells, such as the Vegetable and Cutting Garden next door. Here, David and Criss trial new varieties of edibles such as pumpkins and artichokes, as well as annuals like sunflowers.

David and Criss love experimenting in many ways, from their extraordinary seasonal flower displays to the new plants they create in the nursery. Their brave and inspiring approach shows that, with a little thought and effort, a dry-climate garden can be just as exciting, vibrant, and colorful as any other.

Clockwise
from top left
*Diverse textures,
from spiky to
soft, coexisting
in the gardens*

*Pink statice
(Limonium
peregrinum)
blooming in the
warmer months*

*A water bowl
standing at
the center of
the Vegetable
and Flower
Cutting Garden*

*David and Criss
standing amid
their plantings*

The John Fairey Garden

WHERE *Hempstead, Texas* **WHEN** *Open days and private tours year round; best times to visit for pleasant weather, blooms, and leaf color are March–April and November–December* **SIZE** *39 acres (15.7 hectares)*

When one door closes, another opens. After punishing weather extremes forced John Fairey to rethink a genteel Southern landscape he was cultivating in Texas, he created one of the world's most unusual gardens—a place where global conservation and design converge.

A mecca for globe-trotting botanists who greatly admire its rare collections, the John Fairey Garden is a welcoming wonderland for anyone who loves plants. Its founder, John Gaston Fairey, built his renowned repository of 3,000 flora by focusing on rare and endangered plants from Mexico, the American Southwest and Asia. But he was also an artist—a formally trained painter who studied with some of the giants of American modern art—and this land was his canvas on which to blend dazzling forms, contrasting textures, and harmonious colors.

VISIONARY DESIGN

Fairey taught design at Texas A&M University but was commuting from Houston, more than 90 miles (145 km) away. Wanting to be closer to work, he purchased the first 7 acres (3 hectares) of his property in 1971, charmed by a spring-fed creek and scrubby woodland that reminded him of his boyhood in South Carolina. He set to work creating a garden full of plants he was

familiar with; he lined the creek with bald cypresses and planted camellias and azaleas underneath old oaks. In 1983, however, disaster struck when a tornado sheared the tree canopy and a winter storm shocked what remained. Though devastated, Fairey didn't give up. Rather, he pondered how to create a garden that could withstand the elements. →

FOCUS ON

Woody Lilies

The sculptural beauty of the dry or "woody lily" gardens, which Fairey laid out in the early 1990s, has influenced landscape designers the world over. Technically not lilies because they do not grow from bulbs, this special collection of spiky, spiny, or grassy plants includes species of Manfreda, yucca, agave, Beschorneria, and Hemiphylacus.

Clockwise from top
Yucca rostrata *with its grasslike, spiny textures, among other species*

Hedychium coccineum *flowering in its beautiful orange tones*

The Japanese maple Acer palmatum *"Oridono-nishiki"*

Embracing the fresh palette of altered conditions, Fairey shifted his focus to heat- and drought-tolerant native species that were not yet common. On a mission to investigate and collect new plants, he met legendary plantsman Lynn Lowrey. The two set off on a botanizing expedition to Mexico, with Lowrey introducing Fairey to a whole new world of planting possibilities. Over time, he made more than 100 trips to save plants that were disappearing rapidly from the temperate, semi-arid highlands of the Sierra Madre. This garden bears the fruits of that labor—Fairey raised many of its prized specimens from seeds and cuttings.

AN ARTIST'S GARDEN

The garden grew over the years, with Fairey acquiring more property and cofounding the succulent-centric Yucca Do Nursery with his partner, Carl Schoenfeld. Conservation was put at the heart of the space as he repaired the depleted landscape and introduced new plants. Yet he stayed true to his roots as an artist, at once creating a space that could withstand the elements but was aesthetically pleasing, too.

Expansive outdoor "rooms" are organized by plant types, light, and soil requirements. Oaks native to Mexico and Texas provide the garden's backbone, and the rarest of them reveal surprisingly varied shapes and cast shadows across the long, raised earth of the garden's long oak berm. Beyond the oak berm, in harsh sunlight, Fairey elevated arid-climate plants in smaller berms to help them survive in an environment where drought alternates with torrential rains. These dry gardens are a visual delight, full of beautiful displays of blue-gray agaves, aloes, and sabal palms that Fairey chose for their cool tones, dramatic spikes, and architectural beauty. A disciplined collector, Fairey favored architectural characteristics over blowsy flowers, although many of the plants he collected have their showy moments, and nuanced blooms appear throughout the year.

In the transitional courtyard, vines amble up trellises, and water trickles into a rectangular pool from both sides of a stucco wall that provides permanent color, painted terracotta with purple accents. A few steps away, a rich green tapestry of shade-loving natives in dappled light marks the garden's remaining woodlands. Descending toward the creek is a cleared "hallway," where the moody stubs of cypress trees poke up from roots at the water's edge. A sleek metal bridge leads across the creek to the north garden, where mixed plantings and a vivid blue stucco wall pay homage to the iconic Mexican home of Frida Kahlo and honor Fairey's love of art. In a final, sunny flourish, rare magnolias, conifers, and oaks from the Americas, Asia, Europe, and Africa come into view across a meadowlike arboretum.

A LIVING LEGACY

Fairey continued to hone his masterpiece until his death in 2020. Not everything he planted survived, with a polar vortex storm in early 2021 underscoring newer challenges of climate change and the difficulty of maintaining the garden as he left it. Yet what matters the most is honoring Fairey's artistic vision and drive to experiment, no matter the circumstances.

"John Fairey had an outsized influence on American garden design, particularly as a plant explorer, introducing numerous wild-collected Mexican flora to horticulture."

RANDY TWADDLE, EXECUTIVE DIRECTOR,
THE JOHN FAIREY GARDEN

Clockwise
from top
*Xochimilco's
chinampas
from above*

*A colorful
trajinera
navigating the
waterways*

*A woman
watering
plants in a
Xochimilco
nursery*

Floating Gardens of Xochimilco

WHERE *Xochimilco, Mexico City* **WHEN** *March–April brings a warm and dry period when many flowers come into bloom.* **SIZE** *62.5 acres (25 hectares)*

Visitors flock to the Mexico City district of Xochimilco to see some of the most unusual and ingenious gardens on earth—a network of artificial islands connected by waterways that date back seven centuries to the time of the Aztecs.

Upon settling in the area now occupied by Mexico City around 1325 CE, the Mexica—who Europeans would later call the Aztecs—adopted innovative techniques to reclaim land from the swamps of Lake Texcoco for agriculture. The result was a remarkable system of canals, channels, causeways, and *chinampas*, "floating gardens," made from layer upon layer of fertile soil, mud, and vegetation.

PLACE OF THE FLOWER FIELDS

Today Xochimilco (which translates as "place of the flower fields" in Nahuatl, the language of the Mexica) is listed as a UNESCO World Heritage Site. The *chinampas* are still a central part of the local economy—many are covered with neat plots of vegetables, fragrant herbs, groves of fruit trees, and beds of colorful flowers. To see the *chinampas*, visitors tour the channels on elaborately decorated barges called *trajineras*, passing through nature reserves and one of Latin America's largest plant markets as they go. There is a steady stream of mariachi bands,

food vendors, and flower sellers, which gives the area an infectious energy and festival-like atmosphere. More than anything, you're left with a deep appreciation for the technical prowess, horticultural skills, and imagination of the Mexica, who transformed a waterlogged swamp into productive land using innovative methods that have stood the test of time.

FOCUS ON

Chinampas at Risk

Xochimilco's floating gardens are an important supplier of fruit, vegetables, herbs, and flowers for Mexico City. But growing urbanization poses a serious threat. Conservationists argue that the *chinampas* could be lost by 2057 unless action is taken to protect them.

*An impressive feat:
the Sunken Garden's
vibrant display
of 151 flower beds*

CANADA · NORTH AMERICA

The Butchart Gardens

WHERE *800 Benvenuto Avenue, Brentwood Bay, British Columbia* WHEN *Spring and summer,
when a rainbow of colors from the annual flowers, perennials, and bulbs fill the gardens*
SIZE *Public viewing area: 55 acres (22 hectares); overall estate: 135 acres (55 hectares)*

As Jennie Butchart stood at the top of a depleted limestone quarry looking down, she had a
vision: to turn it into a stunning floral garden. The result was not only a horticultural
masterpiece, but a real success story of reclaiming land.

It was the early 20th century when Jennie and her husband, Robert Butchart, built their family home, an estate on the land between Robert's cement plant and an exhausted quarry. This was a time when the Pacific Northwest was flourishing, and, like many wealthy people of the era, Jennie desired beautiful gardens around her home. The early gardens she built on the estate land were rather traditional—a Japanese garden that sloped to the water's edge of Butchart Cove and a large lawn edged in a perennial border. But the biggest challenge of her layout was what to do with the quarry. Known for her unwavering zest to get things done, Jennie soon developed a plan to transform this eyesore into a place of beauty filled with floral displays, with the help of the workers from Robert's cement plant.

A NEW LEASE OF LIFE

It took 11 years of backbreaking work from 1909 to transform the quarry into the Sunken Garden, a masterpiece of design that is still the most impressive part of the Butchart Gardens today. Instead of removing the rock littering the quarry floor, Jennie had it gathered up and used to form the foundation of the many flower beds. Horses and carts moved tons of topsoil from local farms to build the soil base needed for the plants; trees were meticulously chosen and sited; a small lake was added; and a pile of rock never quarried became a mound to climb for better views. Jennie even transformed the gray stone walls into a hanging garden of ivy, tucking the plants into the nooks and crevices of the walls herself while suspended in a chair by a rope.

The vivid floral displays were the final addition. Jennie's eye for color from her early training as an artist helped her transform this blank canvas of rock into a work of art. She created mass plantings using annuals, biennials, perennials, and flowering shrubs in a rainbow of hues and styles. This is a garden to first view from above and then immerse yourself in as you descend the stairs and walk the floor. →

THE VISION UNFOLDS

For Jennie, every inch of the land had the potential to become a stunning work of art. She transformed the family tennis court into the Italian Garden, tucked behind a wall of manicured yews. A rose garden was installed on the former vegetable garden, where 6,000 roses perfume the air from spring into fall.

The Butcharts didn't set out to build a public garden, but it inevitably became one. Naming their home Benvenuto, Italian for "welcome," reflected their hospitality, which became as well known as their gardens. In the early days, tea was served to all, until visitor numbers swelled to 18,000 in 1915. Through wartime and even into years of declining health, the Butcharts welcomed visitors from around the world who traveled great distances to see their masterpiece.

FLORAL DELIGHTS

When Jennie's family took over the gardens after her death in 1950, they honored the legacy of her much-loved floral displays. A visitor center was built, today a site where flowers are picked daily and put on display to showcase what's in bloom. Indeed, the visual impact of the gardens comes from the sheer number of plants blooming at any one time. If most gardens showcase a few of the same

flower, Jennie's has dozens, if not more, planted together: along paths, in garden beds, suspended in massive window boxes at the family's former home. One walkway is lined with dahlias, lilies, and anemones, another with hydrangeas and peonies. Sun and shade gardens mingle. Neatly trimmed shrubs and many Japanese maples tie it all together.

FOCUS ON

Jennie's Rose

The Rose Garden is the only place where you can see the "Jenny Butchart Rose," since it's not in commercial production. This hybrid tea rose named in her honor was developed by a local rosarian from the cultivars "Miss Canada" and "Fragrant Cloud."

Today, when looking down at Jennie's extensive, colorful gardens, it's hard to believe that this space was once an unsightly gray quarry. The pioneering Butchart Gardens truly are an inspiring example of just what can be done with a derelict piece of land and a creative vision.

Clockwise from right

Stairs leading to a rock mound and lookout over the Sunken Garden

Streams trickling in the Japanese Garden

Rose-laden arches leading into the romantic Rose Garden

TIMELINE OF EVENTS

1904

Robert Butchart builds a cement plant on a quarry and moves into a home nearby with Jennie.

1909

Work on the Sunken Garden begins, completed 11 years later in 1921.

1939

The Butcharts give owner-ship of the garden to their grandson, Robert Ian Ross, on his 21st birthday.

1964

At the 60th anniversary of the garden, the Ross Fountain is installed.

1994

The Canadian Heraldic Authority award a coat of arms to the garden.

2004

The garden is designated a National Historic Site of Canada. First Nations totem poles are placed for the garden's 100th anniversary, a tribute to those who lived on the land before the Butcharts.

Clockwise from left

Masses of dense plants lining a winding path

One of several playful bas-reliefs

Muscular planting lining the garden's stone stairway

IF YOU LIKE THIS

Lunuganga

SRI LANKA · ASIA

The nearby estate of Lunuganga belonged to influential architect Geoffrey Bawa, father of Tropical Modernism and Bevis Bawa's brother. Now run as a boutique hotel, this sweeping garden, punctuated by venerable trees, curious pavilions, and striking viewpoints, is well worth a visit. The two brothers were deeply competitive, and nowhere is this more apparent than in their gardens.

Brief Garden

WHERE *Dharma Town, Bentota* WHEN *Year round, though December–April is best to avoid monsoon seasons* SIZE *5 acres (2 hectares)*

Rising up from the floodplain of the Bentota River is the dreamlike oasis of Brief. The life's work of avant-garde landscape architect and garden maker Bevis Bawa, this gloriously idiosyncratic garden rolls down the hillside in a rhapsody of green.

It's hard not be enchanted by this magical pocket of paradise. When hedonist Bevis Bawa inherited his father's small rubber plantation in 1929, his intention for it was never to fit the mold. After building a house for himself at the property's highest point, he began landscaping whimsical gardens out of 5 acres (2 hectares) of the land, leaving the rest as jungle. If the landscape feels as if it has spilled into the garden of its own accord, it's down to Bawa's expert planting style, where vines creep up walls and greenery envelopes archways.

It took a great deal of labor, and the help of his friend, gardener Arthur van Langenberg, for Bawa to transform the site into an exuberant space. Upon entering, visitors are greeted with graceful vistas redolent of the great Italian villa gardens extending down the hillside from the courtyards and shady pergolas of the house. Yet far from the fussiness of formal European gardens, Bawa's planting style is uniquely strong and muscular, the garden's spaces often defined and framed by dense plantings of a single species. A journey through this vivid foliar landscape reveals flashes of red ginger, swathes of black bat flower, and an array of climbers that clamber over eye-catching urns.

AN ARTISTIC LEGACY

Bawa was not just an expert plantsman; he had an artistic eye, too. In 1956, Australian artist Donald Friend came to stay with him, and the pair added an artistic edge to the garden, most notably in the form of fantastical heads and homoerotic sculptures that dot the land.

TRY IT AT HOME

All in the Details

Brief is all about decorative fine detailing. Add mosaics and botanically imprinted tiles to your garden, and think about the artful placement of figurative pots to draw the eye.

When the garden opened to the public in 1969, it was already famous. A socialite, Bawa would host parties here in the 1950s and '60s, where the likes of Vivien Leigh came to revel in the hedonism of his vision. Admiration and envy even spurred on Bawa's brother to create his own striking garden. Indeed, Brief's eccentricity continues to delight all who visit to this day.

Tokachi Millennium Forest

WHERE *Shimizu, Tokachi region, Hokkaido*   WHEN *May to mid-October; from late September, the woodland foliage is saturated with rich fall color*   SIZE *1,000 acres (400 hectares)*

Set within the foothills of central Hokkaido's Hidaka Mountains is this innovative garden, imbued with natural beauty and shaped by thoughtful narratives. Tokachi shines a light on gardening with sensitivity to the natural world and encourages us to reconnect with nature.

Tokachi Millennium Forest is the vision of forward-thinking Japanese media magnate Mitsushige Hayashi, who, nearly 30 years ago, bought a large swathe of land in the foothills of the Hidaka Mountains on Hokkaido, Japan's most northerly island. His aim was to offset the carbon footprint of his national newspaper business by restoring the land, which had suffered from intensive forestry and agriculture, and make it sustainable for the next thousand years. He named it the Millennium Forest.

But Tokachi is about so much more than a transactional carbon offset; it's about creating a whole new understanding of the world around us. Hayashi's own personal mission was to strengthen the connection between Japanese people—90 percent of whom live in cities—and nature. To achieve this, internationally acclaimed landscape designer Dan Pearson was brought on board to design an ecological park. Pearson got to work, creating a narrative of cohesive spaces. Boarded walkways meander through areas of native forest, productive gardens, and, perhaps Pearson's most notable achievement, the Meadow Garden. Here, drifts of tall grasses dance in the wind and vibrant perennials—many of which are native Japanese species—add a bold touch.

At first glance, Tokachi may seem a world apart from traditional Japanese garden design, but Pearson and head gardener Midori Shintani worked hard to ensure it remained true to its roots. The result is a groundbreaking garden that fuses Eastern and Western design sensibilities, combining a popular naturalistic strand of European garden design with a sensitivity and nuance that is quintessentially Japanese.

FOCUS ON

Satoyama

Satoyama is a Japanese concept that embodies a timeless and measured way for humans to coexist and work in harmony with natural cycles. The concept of *satoyama* remains one of the guiding principles at Tokachi Millennium Forest.

217

Above *Cactus garden in the Sun Pavilion*

Left *Supertree Grove and Skyway illuminated at night*

Next page *The futuristic Supertree Grove seen from above*

Gardens by the Bay

WHERE *Marina Gardens Drive, Marina Bay* **WHEN** *Year round; hours vary by attraction. Weekday mornings are quietest; evening light shows start at 8:45 p.m.*
SIZE *250 acres (101 hectares)*

So much more than a tourist attraction, Gardens by the Bay is a breathtaking celebration of horticultural artistry and innovation and an inspiring example of how sustainable garden design can inform the future of urban planning.

The millions of people who come here annually can't help but be dazzled by this cutting-edge horticultural metropolis. And why wouldn't they be? Its vertiginous skyways, climate-controlled conservatories, human-made mountains, and grove of "super trees" as tall as skyscrapers are a spectacle of innovative garden design.

A GARDEN FOR A GARDEN CITY

In 2006, the government of Singapore opened a competition to landscape design firms around the world. The brief was firm and precise: to design exemplary tropical gardens and to make them the best outdoor recreation space in Singapore. Soon, 77 proposals were submitted by firms from 24 countries. British landscaping firm Grant Associates was named the winner. Ground for Gardens by the Bay was broken in November 2007, and it opened to the public in 2012.

FLORAL INSPIRATION

Home to over 1.5 million plant species, Gardens by the Bay comprises three stunning waterfront gardens spread across a swathe of land that was reclaimed from the sea. The orchid, Singapore's national flower, was embraced as inspiration for the build and is represented in the complex's blueprint, in the elegant lines and curved glass. Meanwhile, the orchid's physiology—its ability to thrive in the most unlikely of places with limited resources—is mirrored in Gardens by the Bay's sophisticated infrastructure for managing energy, water, and waste sustainably. →

163,000

The approximate number of plants that grow on the towering metal "tree trunks" of Supertree Grove in Bay South garden.

EXPLORING THE GARDENS

There is much to see here, so allow plenty of time to explore. Bay South is the largest of the gardens, with three conservatories: the Flower Dome, the world's largest all-glass greenhouse; Floral Fantasy, a veritable fairytale wonderland of colorful floral installations; and the Cloud Forest, home to the world's tallest human-made mountain. Far from any conventional mountain hike, however, the lofty summit of this mist-enshrouded peak is reached by elevator, but you can follow a meandering trail back down to ground level. On the descent, you'll pass orchids, ferns, a cavern, a waterfall, and crystal deposits.

Bay East may be smaller in size, but it's no less glorious. It's noted for its waterfront promenade, interspersed with tropical gardens, where some plants have leaves as big as cars. Serving as a link to the two Bay gardens is Bay Central, accessed directly from downtown Singapore.

A NEW GENERATION OF TREES

The highlight of any visit to Gardens by the Bay is Bay South's Supertree Grove. The redwoods of California are mere stalks compared to these towering structures. They are entirely human-made (concrete foundations and steel rods replace roots and bark), but these super trees are designed to function in much the same way as living trees—they gather rainwater, capture solar energy, and provide shade that naturally cools the grounds. Vertical planting panels on the trunks are alive with bromeliads, ferns, flowering climbers, and orchids. An impressive skyway links the trees, and the very tallest is topped with a lofty observation deck offering panoramic views of the gardens and the city beyond. Stunning by day, every evening the forest becomes a dazzling spectacle of colored lights, a sight to rival even the illuminated city skyline of downtown Singapore.

NATURE, ENHANCED

Such spectacles are plentiful here, but Gardens by the Bay is more than just a showpiece. Here, environmental sustainability and innovation underpin every design decision. A special coating on the glass used in Bay South's three biomes cleverly minimizes the heat generated by the sun while maximizing the light that reaches the plants. Carbon-neutral electricity is generated on-site and powers many of the attractions, and runoff from the plantings is gathered and used to power the zero-carbon cooling and dehumidification system.

Just as in nature, a cycle of growth and regeneration fuels the garden. And once again, human ingenuity and the power of nature prove to be a winning combination. Gardens by the Bay reimagines what our future cityscapes could be and plants the seed of environmental innovation for generations to come.

Visitors descending the Cloud Walk in the Cloud Forest biome

IF YOU LIKE THIS

Little Island

US · NORTH AMERICA

Follow a drawbridge from
Manhattan's Pier 55 onto
this artificial oasis of
greenery and meadow
on the Hudson River.

Monteverde Cloud Forest

COSTA RICA · CENTRAL
AND SOUTH AMERICA

This protected biological
reserve is home to some
26,000 acres (10,500
hectares) of natural cloud
forest, thick with tall trees,
mosses, vines, ferns, and
over 400 species of orchids.

The Floating Gardens of Yongning River

CHINA · ASIA

This series of waterfront
gardens in Taizhou
controls flooding and
attracts numerous
species of birds.

Clockwise
from top
*Experimental
plantings in
front of Dixter's
Tudor house*

*Succulents
thriving in the
summer*

*Zinnias and
other species
growing in the
High Garden*

UK · EUROPE

Great Dixter House and Gardens

WHERE *Northiam, Rye, East Sussex* **WHEN** *May, when the meadows come alive with spring-flowering plants such as tulips and poppies* **SIZE** *6 acres (2.4 hectares)*

Great Dixter would be nothing without the ambition of Christopher Lloyd, the gardener responsible for this pioneering landscape. In his perpetually evolving test bed for new plants and arrangements, Lloyd looked to the future of planting—a legacy that continues today.

Great Dixter was the family home of revered gardener Christopher Lloyd, whose life's work was dedicated to creating one of the world's most exciting and experimental gardens. There is so much to see here—pristine topiary, exuberant borders, natural ponds, and wildflower meadows.

Just 10 miles (16 km) inland from the English south coast, Great Dixter benefits from a mild maritime climate—perfect for ambitious gardening. And ambitious Lloyd was: the complex planting style, fostered by his plant knowledge, features unusual cultivars and experimentation with form and color. Most impressive is the mixing of formality and informality, a new style of planting in Lloyd's day. Today, this style dominates the meadows, where plants are naturalized with orchids, crocuses, and more.

Lloyd's rule-breaking underpinned everything. He was determined to extend the season of interest and keep the garden thriving through late October and beyond, using a changing array of plants with foliage of different kinds. One of the first to embrace the golden-brown hues and seedheads of fall, he rejected "tasteful" color combinations and "fashionable" plants.

Lloyd was also a perceptive garden writer, and his writing and boundary-pushing techniques put Great Dixter on the map of seminal gardens. As a result, the garden has hosted a whirlwind of seminars and symposia that have deeply influenced generations of gardeners.

THE NEXT CHAPTER

Following Lloyd's death, the stewardship passed to Fergus Garrett, who worked alongside Lloyd as head gardener. Lloyd was always looking ahead, and his ambition lives on through Garrett, who constantly reassesses the planting palette of the garden and wider estate with an increasing awareness of its value to biodiversity. He continues to push the boundaries, cementing Great Dixter's place as a garden of the future.

1910

House and outbuildings purchased by architectural historian Nathaniel Lloyd as an agricultural property with land and orchards but virtually no garden.

1947

Christopher (the youngest of Lloyd's six children) gains a degree in horticulture at the University of London.

1954

Christopher starts a nursery specializing in propagating plants he deems unusual.

1992

Fergus Garrett starts as head gardener aged 27, and Dixter's dynamism gains pace.

2006

The Great Dixter Charitable Trust is formed after Lloyd's death. The garden continues to evolve as an educational hub.

2019

Fergus Garret receives the RHS Victoria Medal of Honour, horticulture's highest accolade.

IF YOU LIKE THIS

Philadelphia's Magic Gardens

US · NORTH AMERICA

On an abandoned city lot, mosaic artist Isaiah Zagar used tiles, mirror fragments, and other found items to create a quirky sculpture garden.

Kerala Rock Garden

INDIA · ASIA

Nek Chand's rock garden in Malampuzha was designed in the 1990s as a miniature version of his Chandigarh garden.

Rock Garden of Chandigarh

WHERE *Sector No. 1, Chandigarh, India* **WHEN** *The subtropical climate makes spring or late fall the most pleasant times to visit* **SIZE** *25 acres (10 hectares)*

Visiting the Rock Garden is like entering a child's dream. Created in secret over many years by a single, self-taught artist, it confounds and delights as a truly unique garden that features not plants and flowers but contemporary folk art made from concrete and scrap.

The Rock Garden sits on the edge of Chandigarh, a modernist north Indian city designed in the 1950s as a symbol of the country's independence. Yet this garden provides a glimpse of a different India: the epic battles of Hindu mythology, the concept of *jugaad* (an ingenious use of limited resources), and the value of artisanal skill.

A SINGLE VISION

The garden was the creation of Nek Chand, a low-ranking public works official. Employed on the project to build Chandigarh, he began around 1965 to eke out a small garden beside his workplace, using rocks and discarded materials. His plot grew in size and ambition, becoming what he saw as a fantasy kingdom of sculpted gods and goddesses alongside villagers and animals he remembered from his rural childhood.

Discovered by the authorities in 1973, the garden—an illegal occupation of forested land—was at risk of demolition. But recognition of the garden's value meant it instead opened to the public, with Chand given a salary, labor, and materials to continue its development.

DETRITUS AS ART

From the outset, the Rock Garden was a paean to recycling. Make no mistake—this is not a simple reuse of old stone slabs or plastic pots. Rather, discarded electrical moldings are turned into tactile walls, rusty oil drums become fortress doors, and scrap decorates concrete sculptures of animals. More numerous still are the playfully shaped human figures. Clad in everything from teapot lid hats to gleaming bangle saris, serried ranks of these sculptures seem to march and dance in their displays.

Flowers may not be planted, but nature still makes its home here, where hundreds of birds nest alongside their concrete counterparts. This self-made world is astonishing, the extraordinary organic structures suffusing the entire site with a wonderful sense of life.

Far left *Fantastical armies of sculpted figures filling the garden*

Left *Riverside path winding past one of the park's human-made waterfalls*

Nemo's Garden

WHERE *Via Aurelia, 41-4 Noli, Savona, Liguria* **WHEN** *Summer, when the sun shines through the glass from above* **SIZE** *Each domed biosphere is 21.5 sq ft (2 sq m)*

When chemical engineer Sergio Gamberini's crops began suffering from cold weather, an idea struck: could crops thrive underwater, in the sea's near constant temperature? This idea soon turned into a reality with the creation of the first underwater cultivation of terrestrial plants.

The brainchild of Sergio Gamberini and his family-run Ocean Reef Group, Nemo's Garden is a collection of six experimental underwater greenhouses. The plexiglass bubbles are filled with air, floating but fixed by chains to the sea floor. From a control base on land, everything can be monitored: seed germination, plant growth, air quality, humidity. To visit the garden physically requires scuba gear or a boat, but with cameras located inside the pods, anyone with Wi-Fi can check up on how things are growing.

HOW THE GARDEN GROWS

To keep the biospheres and plants free of mold and disease, the crops—including basil, lettuce, passion flowers, and strawberries—are grown not in traditional potting soil but in organic materials and growing mediums such as coco fiber. These are kept hydrated with the salt-free water that naturally condenses on the inside of the biospheres, where temperatures remain warm. Water collected inside the biospheres is mixed with minerals and fertilizers and then given to the plants, which are all grown hydroponically.

WHY TRY?

There are good reasons to research underwater cultivation of plants. Of course, subaqueous farming has its own challenges, but the extreme temperatures and severe weather conditions on our planet are tempered or avoided when we descend under the surface of the sea. Plus, the fresh water in short supply on earth is abundant in Nemo's bubbles, given the salt-free condensation that forms on the inside of the biospheres.

Nemo's plants thrive in their greenhouses, protected from extremes in temperatures and benefiting from the soft blue light filtered by seawater. On the earth's surface, plants often grow in 70 percent relative humidity, but they seem to do even better in the underwater bubbles, where the humidity ranges from 85 to 97 percent through the day.

With every year that passes, the underwater cultivation of terrestrial plants becomes less a sci-fi story and more a serious experiment of sustainability and agriculture. Before long, it could be time for farmers to drop their shovels and grab their scuba gear.

Top *A diver carrying tomatoes grown in the underwater biospheres, in front of a "Tree of Life" sculpture*

Bottom *Checking on the progress of herbs and plants*

229

Enea Tree Museum

WHERE *Buechstrasse 12, Rapperswil, St. Gallen* **WHEN** *As the sun begins to set, when shadows of the trees play beautifully on the stone walls behind* **SIZE** *18.5 acres (7.5 hectares)*

At the first—and only—tree museum in the world, more than 50 trees represent 25 regional species, all saved by an enterprising Swiss landscape architect and replanted on parkland close by the shores of Lake Zurich. This is a collection that grows in size all on its own.

While some people collect rare orchids or heirloom seeds, Enzo Enea collects mature trees. Given that none of them can fit into a greenhouse or window box, Enea leased a bucolic tract of land owned by an abbey to place the replanted trees he acquires. Each specimen is positioned in front of an imposing stone wall—itself composed of recycled blocks from an Italian quarry—and is both sheltered and framed by the wall as if a work of art in a museum.

SAVING A SPECIES

There is something poignant and wonderfully inspiring about the fact that every tree here was once threatened by the chainsaw. They all come with a compelling backstory of lineage, like the horse chestnut dating from 1902, which was being uprooted for a road-widening program until Enea drove past by chance. On close inspection, the scars of staples once used to affix posters to the bark can still be seen. To ensure that such histories remain visible, uprooting and replanting is a delicate process and often involves moving trees by flatbed truck, then wrapping the limbs and pruning the branches to ensure longstanding health.

It is easy to feel an affection for these trees, which assume the presence of living sculpture on the land. In fact, Enea has augmented his collection with a rotating series of artworks that are cleverly paired with the trees. The sculptures vary from the abstract, with sinuous forms that echo those of the trees to more figurative works.

A UNIQUE COLLECTION

The collected trees, as varied as a Japanese cherry and umbrella pine to a Sargent crab apple and a white pine, all come from the local region, ensuring their ability to flourish in the local climate. Depending on the time of year, they assume different colors and foliage, adapting as any museum's collection does. The overall effect is that of a unique tailored forest, every tree flourishing in its fullest glory.

2013

The year that the garden started curating art from the likes of Jaume Plensa, Sergio Tappa, Stella Hamberg, and Veronica Mar—three years after it was founded.

Clockwise from top
Trees exhibited before stone walls as if in a museum

Tailored plantings bordering paths that trace the garden

Sylvie Fleury's Mushrooms artwork gracing the pristine lawn

UK · EUROPE

Kew Gardens

WHERE *Kew, London* **WHEN** *June to September, to see the herbaceous borders at their best* **SIZE** *300 acres (121 hectares)*

Home to the world's most diverse collection of living plants and internationally renowned for its groundbreaking botanical research, Kew is so much more than a garden; it is a beacon that has been lighting the way in plant science for centuries.

Kew is a veritable paradise for plant lovers. Set on the leafy outskirts of London, it is known the world over for its showpiece borders, magnificent trees, and iconic glasshouses. You could come here every day and still something new would catch the eye or lift the heart. Yet there is more to Kew than beauty, for this is also a center of scientific excellence—a hub where specialists identify, research, and conserve rare plants and fungi and share their knowledge worldwide.

The 18th century was an age of exploration and one that saw a burgeoning interest in plants. Shortly after Kew was established, the naturalist Sir Joseph Banks joined Captain Cook's voyage to the Pacific, bringing back dried samples of more than 1,300 new species to England. Banks became the unofficial director of Kew upon his return and was soon organizing plant-hunting expeditions across the world. He determined that species not yet introduced to Europe should first come to Kew, establishing its place on the international stage.

There are now over 50,000 living plants at Kew, many of them endangered species. It is even home to one of the rarest plants in the world—a cycad (*Encephalartos woodii*), found in 1895 in South Africa. Cycads are dioecious, with separate male and female plants, and this is a lone male; standing before it, it's hard not to feel a tingle of wonder, for this is probably the last of its kind.

Kew is not just about international bounties; its outdoor areas contain species closer to home, too, such as lavenders, lilacs, and roses. There are water features, woodland walks, and eccentric follies. In many ways, this is a grand English garden on the frontline of science.

A LIVING LABORATORY

If anything typifies Kew, it's the magnificent Palm House. This huge iron and glass conservatory was erected to house the tropical plants that were being introduced to Britain in the early 19th century. When completed in 1848, it was the largest of its kind in the world. →

1759

Princess Augusta, mother of King George III, founds a botanic garden in the pleasure grounds at Kew Palace. Her son later merges the land with a neighboring estate at Richmond and the gardens are born.

1772

After Sir Joseph Banks becomes Kew's unofficial director, the gardener and botanist Francis Masson embarks on the first of many expeditions. He brings back seeds and specimens from South Africa and North America.

1848

The Palm House opens, followed by the Temperate House in 1863.

1876

The Jodrell Laboratory is built. Work begins on plant pathology and establishes a tradition of scientific research at Kew.

1939

Vegetables and medicinal plants are grown to keep people fed and provide an alternative to importing food during World War II.

2003

Kew becomes a UNESCO World Heritage Site.

"You can't protect the natural world unless you understand it, and one of the great guardians of the natural world is an institution like [Kew]."

SIR DAVID ATTENBOROUGH

It still dazzles today. Tropical palms, vines, and fruits grow in air that is heavy with humidity. The collection brims with important plants: some threatened in the wild, others that can provide food, spices, timber, and medicines. All species represented are invaluable to sustaining life on earth, from the Madagascar periwinkle *(Catharanthus roseus)* with its valuable anti-cancer properties to the tiny pink fruits of the hairy banana *(Musa velutina)* that are being used in genetic studies.

The Palm House is just one of many stunning conservatories at Kew. The Temperate House, the largest, showcases plants from earth's temperate zones, like the Poor Knights lily *(Xeronema callistemon)* from the uninhabited Poor Knights Islands off New Zealand, or the cabbage tree *(Dendroseris litoralis)* that grows only in the Juan Fernandez Islands of the South Pacific. But this area is not just an exercise in bewilderment. The plants here can survive in conditions only above 50°F (10°C), causing many to be under threat out in the world. This conservatory works to rescue such endangered plants, ensuring they meet their potential to provide solutions to problems like food security and climate change.

THROUGH THE TREES

Indeed, conservation is at the root of much of the work at Kew. There are trees here that are as old as the gardens themselves, many of them rare varieties that can be found nowhere else in Britain. Surrounding the conservatories is the Arboretum, which really became established under the stewardship of the botanist Sir William Hooker, who was appointed Kew's first official director in 1841. His son, Sir Joseph Hooker, expanded the collection, establishing the Pinetum, grouping trees into related species, and laying out the striking Holly Walk, an avenue of mature hollies whose crimson berries are a feast for the eyes—and the birds—in the winter.

FOCUS ON

Saving Seeds

Kew's most important contribution to conserving biodiversity is the Millennium Seed Bank Project. Seeds of nearly every native plant in Britain, as well as thousands from around the world, are stored in an underground vault at Wakehurst Place in Sussex, Kew's wilder sister garden.

The Arboretum is vital for researchers looking to conserve the habitats of trees. Of the 14,000 trees in the garden, every one is a source of knowledge. Cedars, for example, can cope well in both dry summers and harsh winters and could prove to be resilient to climate change. The robust London plane *(Platanus x hispanica)* is another vital specimen here; its flaky mottled bark rids it of airborne pollutants. →

Trees not only clean our air, of course, but also reduce the risk of floods by soaking up rain and cool cities by providing shade. Above all, the trees at Kew are simply fascinating. The largest specimen, a coastal redwood *(Sequoia sempervirens)*, reaches 131 ft (40 m) high. Heritage trees, meanwhile, are impressive for their immense life span, like the Japanese pagoda tree *(Styphnolobium japonicum)*, which was planted in Princess Augusta's original garden around 1762.

FUTURE-PROOFING

Uncovering the secrets of threatened plants is just as important for the future as protecting vital pollinators. Kew is dedicated to this: an extensive natural area filled with wildflowers provides valuable nectar for bees, and long grass areas provide habitats for fauna. Perhaps Kew's most compelling sensory experience comes from The Hive, a 56 ft (17 m) installation. Set in the heart of a wildflower meadow, it recreates the fascinating life of a beehive, where 1,000 LED lights glow with the vibrations of Kew's bees, an activity that is then translated into music.

Looking to the future never stops at Kew. In the Kitchen Garden, researchers experiment with atypical crops, aiming to identify sources of food should our reliable crops be affected by climate change. This possibility seemed to be on English broadcaster and natural historian Sir David Attenborough's mind back in 1985, when he buried a time capsule full of food crop seeds and endangered species in the Princess of Wales Conservatory. Due to be opened in 2085, it may provide the world with what could then be extinct plants or seedlings.

WANDER AND WONDER

For all its educational purposes, Kew is also a satisfying place for plant lovers. Soft-pink cherry blossoms bloom in the spring, and 170 different species of roses perfume the air in the summer. Impressive buildings lend added interest, too, from Kew Palace itself to several follies built to resemble classical temples. Yet, no matter how superb the architecture, nor how picture-perfect the rare plants, to wander Kew's paths is to be inspired to protect the natural world, just as its dedicated researchers have been doing for centuries.

———

TRY IT AT HOME

Protect the Bees

Bees are important pollinators and vital to ecosystems the world over, so do your bit for them by cutting the grass less frequently, letting some of your garden go wild so native plants can thrive, and planting nectar-rich species. If you don't have a garden, even a window box will help.

———

**Clockwise
from top**
*Vibrant trees
surrounding the
Sackler Crossing,
a peaceful
walkway*

*Exploring the
Temperate
House*

*Delicate cherry
blossoms gracing
the garden in the
spring months*

Pha Tad Ke Botanical Garden

WHERE *Luang Prabang* **WHEN** *The monsoon season from June to September, when many of the garden's flowers are in bloom* **SIZE** *28 acres (11.5 hectares)*

What began as a vacation to Luang Prabang for Dutchman Rik Gadella quickly evolved into a passion project that saw the need to protect Laos's ethnobotanical heritage. His bright idea was to found a botanical garden—the nation's first—on the banks of the mighty Mekong.

In a city studded with centuries-old temples and pagodas, it may surprise some visitors to learn that one of Luang Prabang's top cultural attractions—Pha Tad Ke—is less than 15 years old. For this is not your average botanical garden. Committed to documenting the cultural knowledge entwined with the flora of this splendid corner of southeast Asia, this innovative green space offers a refreshing and highly sustainable new way to engage with Lao culture.

He harnessed the expertise of green thumbs from Laos and beyond and soon realized that Pha Tad Ke could be more than a standard pleasure garden. Namely, it could be a living museum that would help preserve the ethnobotanical heritage of Laos, which is increasingly threatened by the nation's rapid modernization. Aptly named after the adjacent mountain, known as "the mountain to unite and resolve," Pha Tad Ke finally opened to the public in 2016.

MORE THAN A GARDEN

After selling his Paris-based arts business and hitting the road, Rik Gadella fell in love with the northern Laos city of Luang Prabang. He decided to look for land on which to build a bungalow and stumbled across Pha Tad Ke—a wild jungle property along the Mekong, once used as a hunting pavilion by the Viceroy of Luang Prabang. Sensing its potential as a community space where people could connect with nature, Gadella's idea for a garden was born.

THE ULTIMATE DAY TRIP

An achingly scenic 15-minute ferry ride from Luang Prabang's historical center takes visitors to this glorious garden, about 1.2 miles (2 km) downstream. Inside its folds, seven themed gardens, an arboretum, and a limestone habitat feature more than 1,500 plant species between them, while a permaculture farm and a cave offer more to explore. Most visitors, however, agree that Pha Tad Ke's *pièce de résistance* is its ethnobotanic garden. →

The sun shining through the trees onto the Pha Tad Ke Botanical Garden, overlooking the glistening Mekong River

> "This is more than a job,
> it's important work for me.
> And not just for me, but for
> my country and for the world."

SITH NITHAPHONE, GENERAL MANAGER, PHA TAD KE

Curated by Biba Vilayleck, a France-based doctor in ethno-linguistics who lived in Laos for a decade, the ethnobotanic garden's 10 themed plots demonstrate the various ways that Laos's rich plant life continues to be used by its Indigenous communities. Plants are crucial for everything—relieving menstrual cramps, dyeing textiles, and even warding off evil spirits. Such knowledge is traditionally passed down orally through generations; today, information panels within the garden conserve this insight.

NURTURING LAOS

Pha Tad Ke is helping not only to safeguard the cultural traditions of Laos but also to conserve its biodiversity and future-proof the livelihoods of Lao farmers, who constitute 70 percent of the population. Designed as an outdoor classroom, Pha Tad Ke's permaculture farm hosts courses for Lao farmers on how to increase their yields via sustainable land management techniques. It has always been Gardella's vision that the courses run within the garden, initially funded by grants, will become self-funded by visitor revenue, including income generated from courses currently in development for tourists. More workshops and ideas have followed. An innovative insect food training program for women helps tackle malnutrition, teaching of the nutritional benefits and farming of insects, which have formed part of the Lao diet for centuries.

FOCUS ON

Elephant Medicine

Laos was originally known as Lan Xang, or the "Land of a Million Elephants." In a nod to its legacy, Pha Tad Ke features a plot of medicinal plants traditionally administered to pachyderms.

Tapping into his art world experience, Gadella—along with the wider Pha Tad Ke team—is developing a creative space on the grounds that will host exhibitions, cultural events, and more. The potential of Pha Tad Ke's future—and, as a result, Laos's—is immense.

Top
A banyan tree by the Limestone Habitat

Bottom
Native orchids thriving in the Orchid Nursery

IF YOU LIKE THIS

Booderee Botanic Gardens

AUSTRALIA · AUSTRALASIA

The only Aboriginal-owned botanic garden in Australia, this New South Wales gem features bush tucker and medicinal plants used by Koori people for millennia.

Bogor Botanic Gardens

INDONESIA · ASIA

Southeast Asia's oldest botanic garden has served as an important research center for horticulture and agriculture since it was established in 1817. Beautiful trees, lawns, and ponds feature here.

241

University of Padua Botanical Garden

WHERE *Via Orto Botanico 15, Padua* **WHEN** *Summer, when the plants are at their peak and hundreds of terracotta pots of frost-sensitive specimens are exhibited in tiny rows* **SIZE** *5 acres (2 hectares)*

Botanical gardens are a firm fixture in the world of gardens today, but the Orto Botanico di Padova set the standard for how medicinal plants were first collected, grown, and studied by botanists at universities. It is here that botanical science was truly born.

Founded in 1545 by the Venetian Republic, this botanical garden is the oldest in the world still in its place of origin. Its purpose was to gather and propagate medicinal plants known as *semplici* (simples), but what became clear early on was that the transportation and study of such plants was, despite their name, anything but simple. By the 16th century, specimens were arriving both dead and alive through the port of Venice from as far away as Asia, and the costs and logistics of procuring and keeping track of them were complex. The need to cultivate living plants as well as create a botanical library and herbarium of dried plants was unavoidable if students were going to study them seriously.

DECEPTIVELY SIMPLE

With its clear design and *raison d'être*, Padua looks and feels like no other. Plants have, of course, come and gone, but the garden feels as if it has remained untouched for centuries. The *hortus cinctus* (circular garden) begins simply enough—a circle containing a square, divided into four equal parts by two paths that meet in the middle. These areas represented the known continents at that time: Europe, Africa, Asia, and America. Geometric patterns made of stone break up each space into beds for single specimens, every plant cared for and labeled. It might seem frightfully symmetrical, but the result is like a perfectly organized library: calm and reassuring.

Many plants that can be found all over Europe were introduced to the continent after passing through Padua. What arrived as botanical rarities became so common that some, like tomatoes, even seem native. The first agaves arrived from Mexico in 1561, lilacs in 1565, potatoes in 1590.

THE GARDEN GROWS

Padua still manages to innovate while retaining its authenticity. In 2014, a modern, high-tech glass house was created to contain the Garden of Biodiversity. It's one of the world's most advanced greenhouses, containing plants in five different climate areas, and produces solar energy used to activate pumps for the circulation of rain water. Padua may not be as showy as those that followed, but its beauty lies in its importance for scientific exchange—one that influenced the world and has the means to continue doing so.

Clockwise from right

Goethe's Palm, the oldest plant in the garden, planted in 1585

A fountain and palms marking the entrance to the botanical garden

Potted cacti soaking up sun rays outside

IF YOU LIKE THIS

Botanical Garden of Pisa

ITALY · EUROPE

Founded in 1543 by the botanist Luca Ghini, this was the first university botanical garden in the world. It is technically not considered the oldest because it was moved in 1563, and then again to its current site near the famous leaning tower and Piazza dei Miracoli, in 1591. Herb gardens, an aquatic plant collection and fountains adorn the space.

Lijiang Hylla Alpine Garden

WHERE *Baisha Town, Lijiang, Yunnan Province* **WHEN** *April, May, October, and November show the garden in bloom* **SIZE** *10 acres (4 hectares)*

A fusion of modern design, folk tradition, and alpine splendor, this pared-back garden is a celebration of the ancient Naxi. It offers a contemporary representation of Naxi culture and tradition amid one of China's most celebrated landscapes.

Clockwise from top
Spectacular views from the terraces of Lijiang Hylla Alpine Garden

Snowmelt flowing along one of the garden's many water channels

Raised wooden walkway encircling Xupai

Lying in the alpine reaches of Lijiang, this alpine garden draws heavily on the region's natural and cultural heritage. Completed in 2020, the contemporary landscape is a living monument to the ethnic Naxi group, a Sino-Tibetan people who have inhabited the foothills of the Himalayas since the 11th century. The garden occupies the traces of a former Naxi village and gathers within its footprint terraced farmland, wild pine forest, and trickling snowmelt pools, along with an on-site boutique hotel. There is a wonderful lightness at play here; low walls, some inset with water channels, create the faintest of frames around the garden's scenes.

TREES AND WATER

Stonemasons and carpenters from the local Naxi ethnic group were employed, and time-worn techniques and textures were used in the garden's construction, while indigenous plants like rhododendrons, irises, and alpine pears have been reintroduced to support the local ecosystem. The Naxi custom of harnessing snowmelt from the mountains is respected gracefully in a water feature called "Three Wells." Its channels and pools are a nod to the way Naxi villages would tap alpine runoff into three tiers; the uppermost for drinking, the middle level for washing and preparing food, and the lowest tier for washing clothes.

The main spectacle, though, is a single oak, known locally as a Xupai, which stands at the heart of the garden. It's reached by a raised boarded walkway that winds like a causeway over an alpine meadow. The tree, believed by the Naxi to have mystical protective qualities, would have served as something of a natural totem to those who lived in the hamlet. Here, it is the focal point of a culturally sensitive landscape that seamlessly blends old and new, demonstrating that the traditional and contemporary can coexist in harmony.

Index

Glossary

Annual A plant that completes its entire life cycle, from seed germination to flower, in a single growing season.

Bas-relief A sculpture that is carved onto a surface to stand out from the background.

Berm A round mound, or hill, of soil built on a level patch of land to block out unsightly views, add a raised element to a garden, or create a focal point.

Biennial A plant that takes two years to complete its life cycle and dies in the second growing season after germination.

Box hedging A row of bushes or shrubs that form a boundary to edge beds, for example.

Climber A plant that climbs using objects or other plants as a support.

Cloud pruning A Japanese technique of training shrubs and trees into shapes that resemble clouds.

Cultivar A plant that has been artificially raised and whose distinguishing characteristics are retained when propagated.

Deciduous A plant that sheds leaves at the end of the growing season and renews them at the start of the next.

Design language A style or scheme that guides the design of something to create a coherent styling system.

Dioecious Plants whose flowers bear the reproductive organs of one sex only.

Epiphyte A plant that grows on another plant without being parasitic and derives its moisture and nutrients from the atmosphere as opposed to by rooting into the soil.

Evergreen Plants that retain foliage for more than one growing season.

Family A plant classification category that groups together related types.

Folly A building constructed purely for decoration that may appear as though it has a real function.

Genus A plant classification category ranked between "family" and "species," in which a group of related species are linked by common characteristics. For example, species of horse chestnut are grouped under the genus *Aesculus*.

Geophyte A perennial plant that propagates in the spring from an organ under the surface of the soil, such as a bulb.

Germination The changes—both physical and chemical—that take place when a seed begins to grow and develop into a plant.

Hardscape The human-made features and architectural materials built into a landscape, such as walls or paths.

Herbaceous Plants that have green stems as opposed to hard, woody stems. Primarily applies to perennials.

Humus The organic residue of decayed vegetable matter found in soil.

Hybrid The offspring of genetically different parents.

Hydroponics The process of growing plants in dilute solutions of nutrients, or any form of soilless culture.

Layer planting A type of interplanting where groups of plants are planted closely together in such a way that they flower in succession.

Mesic A habitat or environment that has a balanced supply of moisture, such as a mesic forest.

Microclimate Atmospheric conditions in a small, restricted area that differs from the climate of the surrounding area.

Mulch A material that is applied to the soil surface in a layer to suppress weeds, preserve moisture, and maintain a cool root temperature.

Naturalize To grow and establish something as if it is in the wild.

New Perennialism A garden movement advocating planting herbaceous perennials and grasses in drifts to create a naturalistic look.

Nursery bed An area used to germinate seeds or grow young plants before planting them in permanent positions.

Parterre A flat area in a garden with enclosed, ornamental beds that are separated by gravel.

This formal arrangement typically includes low-growing plants boxed in by hedging.

Perennial A plant that lives for at least three seasons, such as herbaceous plants and woody shrubs and trees.

Propagation Breeding plant specimens by seed (usually the reproductive parts) or vegetative (asexual, such as the stems and roots) means.

Raceme A group of flowers borne on a single stem.

Rambler A plant that grows up and over walls.

Seedling A young plant that has developed from a seed.

Softscape The living horticultural elements of a garden, including plants, flowers, and shrubs.

Species A plant classification category of closely related, very similar individuals.

Terra firma Dry, solid land, distinguished from the sea or air.

Topiary The art of clipping and training trees and shrubs into myriad shapes, notably of the geometric or elaborate kind.

Weeping standard rose A specific type of rose grafted onto a tree to add height to a garden.

Xerophyte A plant that needs very little water and can survive long periods of intense drought, such as those that live in the desert or snowy regions.

Acknowledgments

Dorling Kindersley would like to thank the following authors for their words:

Clark Anthony Lawrence is an Italy-based American garden writer whose work has been published in *Gardens Illustrated, Garden Design Journal,* and the gardening quarterly *HORTUS.* Between writing, he runs the nonprofit cultural association Reading Retreats in Rural Italy.

Christopher P. Baker is a longtime desert dweller and California and Colombia expert. He's authored more than 30 travel books, and his byline appears regularly in such publications as *BBC Travel, National Geographic Traveler,* and *Travel + Leisure.*

Caroline Bishop is a British freelance journalist and author based in Switzerland. She is the coauthor of *DK Eyewitness Switzerland* (2019) and has written two historical novels. When she's not hanging out with the cows in the Swiss mountains, she writes about her adopted home for travel publications in the UK.

Bee Dawson is a social historian who enjoys writing about people, places, and gardens. She has authored 18 books, including *A History of Gardening in New Zealand,* and writes for publications such as *NZ Gardener.* Bee and her husband live and garden on a windswept hill above Wellington Harbour.

Rebecca Ford is a geographer and award-winning travel writer who regularly contributes to pieces on wildlife, gardens, and landscape history. She also writes guidebooks and has a PhD in the historical and cultural landscapes of watercress.

Mary-Ann Gallagher is a writer and editor based in Barcelona. She loves all things green but swears they don't love her back; still, she seeks out secret gardens in the city and beyond, hoping that one day she'll grow a green thumb. She has authored more than 20 guidebooks.

Hannah Gardner is a garden writer, designer, and horticulturist based in the UK. Hannah has studied as a Daiwa Scholar in Japan and pursues interests in writing, plantsmanship and practical horticulture. She regularly contributes to *Gardens Illustrated* and *The Financial Times.*

Robin Gauldie is a journalist and has contributed to more than 30 travel books, including many DK Eyewitness guides. When not on the road in Europe, he can be found in a tiny urban garden in Edinburgh's sunny docklands.

Taraneh Ghajar Jerven is a wordsmith, explorer, and plant lover. Living in Norway, she has authored many books, including the illustrated atlas *Here Is Norway.* She loves hiking among wildflowers and foraging for wild food.

Molly Glentzer dirties her nails in her Texas garden daily and once grew a book, *Pink Ladies & Crimson Gents: Portraits & Legends of 50 Roses.* She loves writing about culture and gardening, and her stories have appeared in *Food & Wine* and other magazines.

Angelica Gray is a garden writer, historian, and designer who loves to discover the story behind every garden she visits. She is the author of *Gardens of Marrakesh* and writes for magazines such as *Country Life* and *The Pleasure Garden.* She is based in dreamy southwest France.

Melisa Gray-Ward is an Australian writer and podcaster living in Berlin. Her writing, which focuses heavily on design, sustainability, and the environment, has appeared in *i-D, The Planthunter, The Big Issue,* and more.

Simon Griver is an Israel-based journalist and managing editor of *Globes,* an Israeli financial news website. Born in England, he has both written and fact-checked travel guides about Israel.

Larry Hodgson is a freelance garden writer from Canada. Author of more than 60 books and countless articles in magazines and web pages, he also writes a daily gardening blog at www.laidbackgardener.blog. His passion is visiting other people's gardens so he can enjoy the beauty without having to do all the work.

Beverly Hurley lives in North Carolina and is the editor of www.gardendestinations.com and North Carolina's *Triangle Gardener* magazine. When she's not gardening, she's visiting other gardens around the world.

Kathy Jentz is editor and publisher of the award-winning *Washington Gardener* magazine. A lifelong gardener, Kathy is also the host of the GardenDC Podcast and coauthor of *The Urban Garden: 101 Ways to Grow Food and Beauty in the City.*

Yoko Kawaguchi is a cultural historian who writes and lectures on Japanese gardens and other aspects of Japanese culture. Her publications include *Japanese Zen Gardens, Authentic Japanese Gardens,* and *Butterfly's Sisters: The Geisha in Western Culture.* She is also actively involved in the Japanese Garden Society in the UK.

Abra Lee is a speaker, writer, and founder of Conquer the Soil: a platform that covers the history, folklore, and art of horticulture. She has spent a lot of time in the dirt as a municipal arborist and airport landscape manager and has been featured in publications such as *The New York Times.*

Stephanie Mahon is the editor of *Gardens Illustrated* and a two-time recipient of the Garden Media Guild Journalist of the Year award. She has written for many publications and has authored gardening guides. She lives in Wales, where she is attempting to create a garden on a steeply sloping, north-facing plot.

David Masello is an essayist, poet, playwright, and feature writer who has lived and worked in New York for decades. He is executive editor of *Milieu* magazine and the author of three books about art and architecture. He can often be seen cycling around Manhattan in search of new gardens to explore.

Claire Masset worked as a gardens editor on *The English Garden* magazine before becoming a publisher for the National Trust. She has authored many books, including *Secret Gardens of the National Trust*. She lives and gardens in Oxfordshire but goes back to her native France whenever she can.

Shafik Meghji is an award-winning travel writer, journalist, and author. Specializing in Latin America and South Asia, he writes for publications such as *BBC Travel* and *Wanderlust*, has coauthored more than 40 guidebooks, and talks about travel on TV, radio, and podcasts.

Thomas O'Malley is an East Asia specialist and regular contributor to guidebooks. If he's not reviewing hotels for *The Telegraph*, he's probably working on his first novel, which might just feature a Chinese garden.

Sarah Reid is an Australian travel writer, editor, and sustainable travel expert. She has visited more than 120 countries to research features for the likes of *BBC Travel*, *Adventure.com*, *Nat Geo Travel*, *Qantas* magazine, and more. When she's not traveling, she's planning her next positive-impact adventure.

Advolly Richmond is a garden, landscape, and social historian. A member of the Garden Media Guild, she is a garden history television presenter on BBC *Gardener's World* and is a contributor on plant history for BBC *Gardener's Question Time*. She lectures on a variety of 16th–20th-century topics and produces *The Garden History* podcast.

Tony Spencer is the Canadian writer, photographer, speaker, and planting designer behind *The New Perennialist*, an influential blog about naturalistic planting design. His work is recognized with awards from GardenComm and the Perennial Plant Association. He can usually be found experimenting on wild-ish gardens in the hills of Ontario.

Daniel Stables is a travel writer and journalist based in Manchester. He writes for many print and online publications and has authored or contributed to more than 30 travel books on destinations across Asia, Europe, and the Americas.

Jennifer Stackhouse is an Australian horticulturist and writer. She has written and edited many gardening books (including the award-winning title *Garden*) and is a contributor to local radio, newspaper, magazines, and websites. Jennifer lives Tasmania, with a large country garden and a menagerie of pets.

Agnes Stevenson is a journalist, gardening writer, and editor of *Scottish Gardener Magazine*. She also writes for publications in the UK and overseas. When not visiting other people's gardens, she can be found in her greenhouse or tumbling down the steep slope in southwest Scotland that she is attempting to turn into a horticultural paradise.

Lisa Voormeij, originally from the Netherlands and now residing in British Columbia, is a regular contributor to DK Eyewitness guidebooks. If she's not in Canada, she's likely in Hawaii hiking the rainforests and indulging in sushi.

Jane Wrigglesworth is a writer, editor, and longtime gardener. She writes for several gardening and lifestyle magazines, including *NZ Gardener*. She is also the founder of www.sweetliving magazine.co.nz, a free online lifestyle magazine, and www. flamingpetal.co.nz, a blog on growing flowers.

About the illustrator:

Maggie Enterrios is a California-based illustrator and author, whose books include *Flowerscape: A Botanical Coloring Book*. Maggie's ornate botanical artwork can be found on product packaging, books, and textiles around the world. She particularly loves both drawing and growing fuschia.

Main references:

p49 pull quote: Vere Boyle, E. (1900) *Seven Gardens and a Palace*. 1st edn. London: John Lane.

p55 pull quote: Cain, M. (2019). National Trust press release, *Sissinghurst Castle Garden welcomes winter visitors for the first time*. [Online]. Available at: https://www.nationaltrust.org.uk/ press-release/sissinghurst-castle-garden-welcomes-winter-visitors-for-the-first-time. (Accessed: 17 December 2021)

p75 column 1, lines 15–16: Bloedel, P. (Spring 1980). "The Bloedel Reserve: Its Purpose and Its Future," *University of Washington Arboretum Bulletin*, 43 (1).

p100 pull quote: Jencks, C. (2003) *The Garden of Cosmic Speculation*. 1st edn. London: Frances Lincoln Ltd, p17.

p126 pull quote: Herner, I. (2014). "Edward James and Plutarco Gastélum in Xilita: Critical Paranoia in the Mexican Jungle," *Journal of Surrealism and the Americas*, 8 (1), p110.

p134 column 1, lines 6–7: Walska, G. (1943) *Always Room at the Top*. 1st edn. New York: Richard R. Smith.

p154 pull quote: Wilczek, E. (1895) (cited in a commemorative booklet *Centenaire de la Thomasia, jardin alpin de Pont de Nant*, 1991, and translated from French).

p162 pull quote: Oudolf, P. (2021). Provided by Piet Oudolf to DK.

p173 column 1, line 11: Slatalla, M. (2013) "The Best Secret Garden in Barcelona," *Gardenista* (Issue 85—Travels with an Editor: Barcelona), 12 August [online]. Available at: www.gardenista. com/posts/palo-alto-barcelona. (Accessed: December 13, 2021)

p207 pull quote: Twaddle, R. (2021). Provided by Randy Twaddle to DK.

p234 pull quote: *Kew Gardens - The Breathing Planet Campaign* (2013) YouTube video, added by Royal Botanic Gardens, Kew. [Online]. Available at: https:// www.youtube.com/watch?v=g4-EkRL-J2M (0:19–0:28). (Accessed: 17 December, 2021)

p240 pull quote: Nithaphone, S. (2013). *Pha Tad Ke Botanical Garden Newsletter*, 10 [online]. Available at: www.pha-tad-ke. com/wp-content/uploads/ 2016/10/Newsletter-PTK-10E.pdf. (Accessed: December 13, 2021)

Dorling Kindersley would like to thank the following for their kind permission to reproduce their photographs:

(Key: a-above; b-below/bottom; c-center; f-far; l-left; r-right; t-top)

2-3 Claire Takacs. 6 Alamy Stock Photo: Derek Teo (bl); John Norman (tl); Jon Arnold Images Ltd (tr). **Clive Nichols:** (br). **7 Claire Takacs. 12-13 Getty Images:** ivanreinaramirez / 500px (c). **14 Alamy Stock Photo:** Angus McComiskey (t). **Unsplash:** Jan Zinnbauer (b). **17 Alamy Stock Photo:** H-AB (br). **Shutterstock.com:** junjun (tl); Kiev.Victor (tr); lotsostock (bl). **18-19 Getty Images / iStock:** loonger. **21 Alamy Stock Photo:** Best View Stock (tr); ZhenZhang (tl); Natalia Lukiianova (b). **22 Alamy Stock Photo:** Hilda DeSanctis. **24 Shutterstock. com:** Zarrina. **25 Garden Exposures Photo Library:** Andrea Jones (r). **Getty Images:** Richard T. Nowitz (l). **27 Alamy Stock Photo:** travelib india (b, tr). **28 Clive Nichols:** (t, b). **31 Alamy Stock Photo:** Britain - gardens and flowers (tl); Nick Scott (tr); Mieneke Andeweg-van Rijn (b). **33 Getty Images.** : Mint Images (tl); Tom Schwabel / Moment (tr). **Shutterstock.com:** Michael Warwick (b). **35 Garden Exposures Photo Library:** Andrea Jones / courtesy Powerscourt (b, t). **37 Getty Images:** gong hangxu (l); Waitforlight (r). **38 Alamy Stock Photo:** Hao Wan (r). **Shutterstock.com:** Anton_ Ivanov (l). **39 Alamy Stock Photo:** avada. **41 Keukenhof:** (bl, br); Laurens Lindhout (t). **42 Lars Gerhardts/HMTG. 45 Alamy Stock Photo:** Image Professionals GmbH (tl); Jurate Buiviene; mauritius images GmbH (b). **47 123RF.com:** Marco Rubino. **48 Alamy Stock Photo:** Valerio Mei (r). **Dreamstime.com:** Stefano Valeri (tl). **GAP Photos:** Matteo Carassale (bl). **50 National Trust Images:** Andrew Butler (b); Jonathan Buckley (t). **52-53 National Trust Images:** Andrew Butler. **54 National Trust Images:** Andrew Butler (bl, r); Jonathan Buckley (tl). **57 Clive Nichols. 58 Alamy Stock Photo:** Mehdi33300 (r). **Getty Images:** Shaun Egan / DigitalVision (l). **61 Alamy Stock Photo:** Jerónimo Alba (br); Perry van Munster (bl). **Getty Images:** Michele Falzone / Stockbyte (t). **62 Shutterstock.com:** SJ Travel Photo and Video. **65 Alamy Stock Photo:** Adam Eastland (tr); Simona Abbondio (b). **Dreamstime.com:** Giuseppemasci (tl). **67 GAP Photos:** Claire Takacs (tl). **Garden Exposures Photo Library:** Andrea Jones (tr, b). **73 Getty Images:** Melissa Tse (t); Saha Entertainment (b). **74 Marianne Majerus Garden Images:** Marianne Majerus. **77 Courtesy of Bloedel Reserve:** (tr). **Marianne Majerus Garden Images:** Marianne Majerus (tl, bl, br). **79 Getty Images:** Wolfgang Kaehler / LightRocket. **80-81 Alamy Stock Photo:** Danita Delimont. **82 Getty Images:** Wolfgang Kaehler / LightRocket (l, r). **83 Shutterstock.com:** Ian Atwood. **85 Alamy Stock Photo:** Alex Ramsay (tr); Sean Pavone (b). **Getty Images:** Zhang Peng / LightRocket (tl). **86 Getty Images:** Yann Berry. **89 Alamy Stock Photo:** Alex Ramsay (t); beibaoke (b). **91 Alamy Stock Photo:** MLouisphotography. **92 Alamy Stock Photo:** Glenn Harper (tl); travelib europe (bl); Terry Smith Images (r). **95 Alamy Stock Photo:** Yuriy Chertok (b). **Shutterstock. com:** Oleg Bakhirev (t). **97 Getty Images / iStock:** Fotofantastika (b); MagioreStock (tr); svarshik (tl). **99 Alamy Stock Photo:** gardenpics (b). **Garden Exposures Photo Library:** Andrea Jones (t). **103 Daniel Shipp:** (tr, l). **104 Fondazione Walton. 107 Alamy Stock Photo:** Arcaid Images (bl). **Fondazione Walton:** (br). **Getty Images:** Lonely Planet (tr). **Shutterstock.com:** Mazerath (tl). **109 GAP Photos:** Lynn Keddie (r). **Garden Exposures Photo Library:** Andrea Jones (l). **111 Alamy Stock Photo:** AnneyLier (t, br). **Shutterstock.com:** Anney_ Lier (bl). **117 Chris Coad Photography:** (tl, tr, b). **119 Hermannshof:** . **120 Hermannshof:** Claire Takacs (bl) (tl). **Marianne Majerus Garden Images:** MMGI / Marianne Majerus (tr). **121 Hermannshof:** (br). **122 Shutterstock.com:** Tatyana Mut (tr, tl, b). **125 Alamy Stock Photo:** Alfredo Matus. **129 Alamy Stock Photo:** Aeoliak (br); Barna Tanko (tr). **Shutterstock.com:** Nailotl (l). **131 Used with permission from The Biltmore Company, Asheville, North Carolina. 132 GAP Photos:** Karen Chapman. **133 Alamy Stock Photo:** Anne Rippy (l). **GAP Photos:** Karen Chapman (r). **135 Lotusland:** Kim Baile (t, br, bl). **136 GAP Photos:** Matteo Carassale. **139 Alamy Stock Photo:** Allen Brown (t). **GAP Photos:** Matteo Carassale (b). **140 GAP Photos:** Matteo Carassale (tl, r); Neil Overy (bl). **142 Claire Takacs:** (t, b). **144-145 Claire Takacs. 147 GAP Photos:** Helen Harrison (t, bl, br). **149 Desert Botanical Garden:** (b); Adam Rodriguez (tr, tl). **150 Desert Botanical Garden:** Adam Rodriguez (l, r). **151 Desert Botanical Garden. 152 GAP Photos:** Benedikt Dittli. **155 GAP Photos:** Benedikt Dittli (tr, tl, br, bl). **156-157 Getty Images / iStock:** aizram18. **158 Alamy Stock Photo:** Alex Ramsay (tl). **The Garden Collection:** Sibylle Pietrek (bl, r). **160 Garden Exposures Photo Library:** Andrea Jones (bl). **161 The High Line. Photo by Timothy Schenck. Courtesy of the High Line:** Timothy Schenck (t, br). **164-165 The High Line. Photo by Timothy Schenck. Courtesy of the High Line:** Timothy Schenck. **171 Alamy**

Stock Photo: Christine Wehrmeier (tr). **The Garden Collection:** Derek Harris (tl). **Getty Images / iStock:** miroslav_1 (b). **172 Alamy Stock Photo:** Anton Dos Ventos. **175 Shutterstock. com:** haveseen (t, b). **177 Shutterstock.com:** Mariano Luis Fraga. **179 Shutterstock. com:** Fausto Riolo; Luis Echeverri Urrea (b). **181 Alamy Stock Photo:** Lazyllama (tr); Nathaniel Noir (tl). **Shutterstock.com:** oksanatukane (b). **183 Alamy Stock Photo:** ILYA GENKIN (t). **Shutterstock.com:** Jirayu Phaethongkham (b). **184-185 Unsplash:** Darren Nunis (c). **186-187 Alamy Stock Photo:** Feline Lim / Reuters. **189 GAP Photos:** Sarah Cuttle (t, bl, br). **190 Getty Images / iStock:** Nirad (b). **Shutterstock.com:** Distinctive Shots (t). **193 Alamy Stock Photo:** chrispictures (b); Hans Winke (tr); Henryk Kotowski (tl). **198-199 Eden Project, UK:** Hufton+Crow. **201 Alamy Stock Photo:** Martin Bennett (br). **Eden Project, UK:** (tr); Hufton+Crow (l). **203 Annette O'Brien for the Design Files:** (tl, tr, bl, br). **204 Courtesy The John Fairey Garden Conservation Foundation:** (bl, br). **208 Getty Images:** Gianfranco Vivi (t). **Shutterstock.com:** Everton Bento (br); Teran Studios (bl). **210 Alamy Stock Photo:** Dave Mitchell Images. **213 Getty Images:** traveler1116 / E+ (b); Wolfgang Kaehler / LightRocket (tl). **Getty Images / iStock:**

wwing / E+ (tr). **214 Dominic Sansoni:** (tl, tr, b). **217 Tokachi Millenium Forest:** Kiichi Noro (b); Syogo Oizumi (t). **218 GAP Photos:** Andrea Jones (tr). **Unsplash:** Hu Chen (l). **220-221 Unsplash:** Sergio Sala. **223 Unsplash:** Miguel Sousa. **225 GAP Photos:** Abigail Rex (t); Jonathan Buckley (br, bl). **226 Alamy Stock Photo:** Ben Pipe. **Shutterstock.com:** saiko3p (r). **229 Getty Images:** Alexis Rosenfeld (t, b). **231 Enea Tree Museum:** Enea Tree Museum (t, br, bl). **233 Clive Nichols:** . **236 Alamy Stock Photo:** Wirestock, Inc. (br). **237 Alamy Stock Photo:** Steve Tulley (b). Marianne Majerus **Garden Images:** MMGI / Marianne Majerus (t). **239 Pha Tad Ke Botanical Garden:** Cyril Eberle. **241 Pha Tad Ke Botanical Garden:** Cyril Eberle (t); PTK (b). **243 Alamy Stock Photo:** Hilke Maunder (tr); Philipp Zechner (tl). **Getty Images:** LYSVIK PHOTOS / Moment Open (b). **244 Z'scape:** (t, bl, br)

All other images © Dorling Kindersley

Project Editors Zoë Rutland, Danielle Watt
Senior Designers Tania Da Silva Gomes, Ben Hinks
Senior Editor Alison McGill
US Editor Jennette ElNaggar
Designer Jordan Lambley
Proofreader Stephanie Smith
Indexer Helen Peters
Picture Researcher Jackie Swanson
Jacket Designer Tania Da Silva Gomes
Jacket Illustrator Maggie Enterrios
Senior Production Editor Jason Little
Technical Prepress Manager Tom Morse
Senior Production Controller Samantha Cross
Managing Editor Hollie Teague
Managing Art Editor Bess Daly
Art Director Maxine Pedliham
Publishing Director Georgina Dee

First American Edition, 2022
Published in the United States by DK Publishing
1450 Broadway, Suite 801, New York, NY 10018

MIX
Paper from
responsible sources
FSC™ C018179

This book was made with Forest Stewardship Council ™ certified paper—one small step in DK's commitment to a sustainable future. For more information go to www.dk.com/our-green-pledge

The rapid rate at which the world is changing is constantly keeping the DK Eyewitness team on our toes. While we've worked hard to ensure that *Gardens of the World* is accurate and up-to-date, we know that garden events are liable to change and plant displays are influenced by many variables, not least the weather. If you notice we've got something wrong or left something out, we want to hear about it. Please get in touch at travelguides@dk.co.uk